"A perfect book for this moment. What Eric Loucks teaches is highly calibrated for young people to effectively navigate the steep c'' ╎ that are intrinsically healing, liberating, and sore⌐ ╎ the future of humanity and the planet amid the h╎ ╎ es of this Anthropocene Age. And for that reason ╎ ╎ nor-mously from inviting even a few of these extre ╎ ╎ ind-fulness practices into one's life."

> —**Jon Kabat-Zinn**, founder of mindfulness-based stress reduction (MBSR), and author of *Meditation Is Not What You Think* and *Mindfulness for All*

"At a time of growing concern over stress and anxiety among our college students, *The Mindful College Student* offers young adults and readers of all ages a powerful guide to navigating everyday challenges through an evidence-informed approach to mindfulness. With insightful techniques to reinvigorate your life by improving your health, well-being, and performance, this important book is a gift that will keep on giving—on campus and beyond."

> —**Tim Ryan**, United States Congressman from Ohio, and author of *A Mindful Nation* and *Healing America*

"This book gives such creatively workable adaptations of traditional Buddhist mindfulness techniques. Because of the author's considerable experience of teaching mindfulness personally, it stays well-rounded and friendly; good, real-life stories stress the cheerful balance of the 'middle way.' I would have liked to have found something like this when I was younger—it should help many college students in their new life."

> —**Sarah Shaw**, tutor at the University of Oxford, fellow of the Oxford Centre for Buddhist Studies, and author of *Mindfulness*

"An inspiring exploration of how mindfulness can support the commonly turbulent transition into adulthood. It offers a systematic road map to both integrating mindfulness into small daily micro-moments, and into the bigger dilemmas particular to this life stage. Young people will reap the benefits throughout their life. Importantly, engaging with this approach will enable freedom to pursue life directions which play to their unique strengths and passions, and this will undoubtedly benefit all beings."

> —**Rebecca Crane, PhD**, director at the Centre for Mindfulness Research and Practice at Bangor University, author of *Mindfulness-Based Cognitive Therapy*; and coeditor of *Essential Resources for Mindfulness Teachers*

"It would have been so helpful to have *The Mindful College Student* during my college years. In this comprehensive work, Eric Loucks lays out a program of mindfulness training that touches on every aspect of our lives. He engages the reader with probing questions of self-inquiry, and offers many practical exercises for deepening our understanding. A wonderful contribution to the well-being of both college students and us all."

> —**Joseph Goldstein**, author of *Mindfulness*

"College is an exciting time filled with new opportunities, health risks, and stress, while the potential for deep personal transformation and self-knowledge is ripe to be discovered. As an expert scientist and skilled mindfulness teacher, Eric Loucks helps readers realize the possibility of choosing a more mindful college experience. Loucks skillfully brings together ancient practices, personal experience, and modern wisdom to lay out a path for students toward greater self-regulation, which offers them more control over their college experience and life beyond. As you pack to head off for college or graduate school, this is one book you will be glad that you brought along."

—**Zev Schuman-Olivier, MD**, director of the Center for Mindfulness and Compassion, and director of addiction research at Cambridge Health Alliance; and assistant professor of psychiatry at Harvard Medical School

"College is a formative time—we learn how to relate to others, we develop work habits, we take responsibility for our health, we explore sexuality, and we develop our aspirations beyond graduation. Drawing on ancient wisdom and modern psychology, this book provides college students with a compass, a map, and ways to develop skills that help them through these early adult years. More than this, it teaches them how to navigate their lives aligned with their values, and with awareness imbued with qualities of curiosity, kindness, and care— in ways that impact their world positively. It is a brilliant distillation of deep understanding, scientific evidence, and extensive experience of what works into something that college students can use not only in college, but also throughout their lives. This is no surprise given the author's clarity of vision; exemplary career as a writer, teacher, and scientist; and long, personal training in mindfulness."

—**Willem Kuyken**, Ritblat Professor of mindfulness and psychological science at the University of Oxford

"This book is a great resource to help students flourish during the challenging time of college. It is replete with simple, short, practical meditation exercises that can reduce distractibility, improve focus, and clarify values. And sprinkled throughout are tidbits to ground the recommendations in evidence-based science. This book is a must-read for every college student wishing to succeed in life, and will be useful for just about everyone else."

—**Richard J. Davidson**, coauthor of *Altered Traits*, and founder and director of the Center for Healthy Minds at University of Wisconsin-Madison

"What would happen if someone offered you a tool kit and said that within it you would find a path to less suffering? *The Mindful College Student* is an introspective weaving of shared experiences, the science of mindfulness practices, and some words of wisdom from the Buddha. Eric Loucks describes how to find a way forward through any kind of circumstance that arises in life."

—**Sharon Salzberg**, author of *Lovingkindness* and *Real Change*

The Mindful

COLLEGE

STUDENT

HOW TO SUCCEED,
BOOST WELL-BEING &
BUILD THE LIFE YOU WANT
AT UNIVERSITY & BEYOND

ERIC B. LOUCKS, PHD

FOREWORD BY
JUDSON A. BREWER, MD, PHD

Statement on Confidentiality

In some of the stories in this book, I changed the names of people to protect their privacy.

Limit of Liability

While the publisher and author have used their best efforts in preparing this book to provide accurate information in regard to the subject matter covered, the advice and practices contained in it may not be suitable for your situation. You should consult with a professional where appropriate. Neither the publisher nor the author shall be liable for any damage.

Distributed in Canada by Raincoast Books

NEW HARBINGER PUBLICATIONS is a registered trademark of New Harbinger Publications, Inc.

Copyright © 2022 by Eric B. Loucks
New Harbinger Publications, Inc.
5674 Shattuck Avenue
Oakland, CA 94609
www.newharbinger.com

The Mindfulness-Based College curriculum was developed at and is copyrighted by Brown University. Excerpts are used by permission from Brown University.

Mindfulness-Based College for Young Adults (MBC) Curriculum and Teaching Guide Copyright © 2021 by Brown University. All rights reserved.

Cover design by Sara Christian; Acquired by Elizabeth Hollis Hansen; Edited by Gretel Hakanson

All Rights Reserved

Library of Congress Cataloging-in-Publication Data

Names: Loucks, Eric B., author.
Title: The mindful college student : how to succeed, boost well-being, and build the life you want at university and beyond / by Eric B. Loucks.
Description: Oakland, CA : New Harbinger Publications, [2022] | Includes bibliographical references.
Identifiers: LCCN 2021052631 | ISBN 9781684039135 (trade paperback)
Subjects: LCSH: College students--Psychology. | College students--Conduct of life. | Mindfulness (Psychology)
Classification: LCC LB3609 .L68 2022 | DDC 378.1/98--dc23/eng/20220125
LC record available at https://lccn.loc.gov/2021052631

Printed in the United States of America

24   23   22

10   9   8   7   6   5   4   3   2   1   First Printing

The Haudenosaunee Confederacy (Iroquois) is attributed to considering how important it is that we reflect on the ways our actions today will impact seven generations in the future. This book is dedicated to the next seven generations, starting with the first, including my children, Stella and Monica, and all young adults at this moment in history.

Contents

Foreword

As a psychiatrist, I am always looking for the best ways to help my patients work with and overcome mental struggles, ranging from addiction to anxiety. As a neuroscientist, I'm endlessly intrigued by how the mind works, and how to translate new discoveries into my clinical practice. And as a professor in the School of Public Health at Brown University, I get to explore all of these concepts with my university students—with the goal of my students trying them out in their daily lives with lasting effects.

Whether I'm working with patients in my clinic, or students in my classroom, I'm constantly amazed how there is no primer course for life entitled, "This Is How Your Brain Works. And This Is How To Work With Your Brain." The closest I ever got to such a course in college was a class with the generic-sounding title "Brain 101." I still remember being fascinated by the subject matter, but looking back, it had a very objective feel to it. I learned a lot about scientific experiments in rats, pigeons, and humans that pointed to some concepts that made sense, but the class never helped me put these concepts into practice. In medical school, I started meditating. This hands-on approach to my own mind helped me start to connect the dots between theory and real life. And it changed my life, literally.

Meditation helped provide that "still point," as T. S. Eliot put it, in a constantly moving world. With the vantage point of not being constantly shaken and stirred up, I could start to see how my mind worked, and from there, start to work with it. Learning to meditate was so powerful and helpful that I shifted the focus of my research career to studying it, and became a psychiatrist so I could apply it with the hopes of helping others. Yet, this was something I did outside of school, in my own elective on life.

"Mindfulness-Based College" is the course I wish I had access to as a college student. And Eric Loucks is the professor I wish had taught it.

Eric and I have been friends for about a decade. We first met in shared research circles, skipping stuffy talks at conferences to spend time poolside, geeking out about meditation practice—how to study it and how to bring it to life by developing new treatments based on its foundational elements. A few years ago Eric dangled a tasty-looking carrot: "If you moved your lab to Brown and joined our Mindfulness Center, I could teach you how to surf." "Sign me up!" How could anyone decline such a delicious offer? Of course, there were many other considerations to my team and the field that he and I made alongside the move to Brown. But still, I can remember that giddy feeling the first time we pulled up to the beach, Eric walking me through the basics of how to "pop up" on a surfboard. He has a natural ease and calmness that he brings with him, from the classroom to the water—one born from a consistent mindfulness practice. And with it, whether helping me learn to catch a wave or helping a student grasp a difficult concept, he teaches with a clarity that is constantly infused with curiosity.

The tricky part about mindfulness is that the concepts only go so far. Concepts provide a useful and needed framework that can point us in a certain direction, but we still have to walk that path ourselves. Only from this experience can we develop the wisdom to navigate our own lives. It is likely because Eric has long walked this path himself that he has been able to develop a deeply meaningful course for college students (and study it with huge effects!). He has distilled that course into an essential book that any young adult can use as a way to chart their own path toward calm and clarity and connection.

In a world that seems to be sprouting new sources of uncertainty on a daily basis, I have witnessed first hand—in my clinic, in my classroom, and in my research studies—a natural tendency to turn away, distract, or shut ourselves down to the environment around us. This is a natural protective mechanism that is meant to help us survive. Yet, ironically, this closed-down, contracted way of being makes it harder for us to interact with others in the present moment and to plan for the future. It leads to anxiety and unhealthy coping mechanisms such as drinking too much, spending too much time on social media, or binging on our favorite television show.

The Mindful College Student does something different. It teaches us to open ourselves to ourselves and our world. Through stories, examples, and pragmatic tools that we all can put into practice, this book provides step-by-step instructions for how to open our bodies, our hearts, our minds, and our spirits. In fact, *The Mindful College Student* goes even further than that. It helps us chart our own career and life paths so that we can skillfully and creatively navigate our surroundings in our social, political, and physical environments.

Eric's intention for this book is clear: to provide a cohesive framework for anyone who reads it to have the skills and tools to foster a lifelong well-being for themselves and the lives they touch. Bringing together science, ancient teachings, and his own direct experience—personal and professional—Eric has written the essential "how to" guide for any young adult looking to navigate their inner and outer world as they move through life.

—Judson Brewer MD, PhD
October, 2021

Is This a Good Time to Engage in Mindfulness and Meditation Practices?

Meditation involves coming closer to our thoughts, feelings, and physical sensations. This can sometimes be uncomfortable. If you have a psychiatric challenge, such as trauma, post-traumatic stress disorder (PTSD), psychosis, depression, anxiety, or bipolar disorder, this may be a difficult time to engage in learning mindfulness and meditation. There is evidence supporting that mindfulness trainings can help with all of these health challenges, but sometimes in a particular adapted way for the specific condition (see, for example, Treleaven 2018; Kuyken et al. 2016; de Vibe et al. 2017; Gaudiano et al. 2020). You might like to talk with your doctor or mental health provider to see if now is a good time to engage in mindfulness and meditation training, and if so, if they have recommendations. As you read this book, I encourage you to notice how the mindfulness and meditation practices feel to you. If they are helpful, then keep using them. If they aren't, then let them go. There are many paths to health and happiness.

Introduction

If you have picked up this book, there is a good chance that you are a young adult—possibly a college or university student, but it's fine if you're not. In fact, it's fine if you're not a young adult. The research and the lessons in this book apply across the adult life span. However, the reason this book is geared toward young adults is that I believe this is one of the most powerful times in life to learn mindfulness. My mindfulness research in young adults, which this book is grounded in, and the stories from young adults that fill the book testify to this moment in life being a remarkable time to learn mindfulness and apply it. I have seen countless college students and young adults for which mindfulness training changed their lives. It's because of this, along with the fact I was lucky to receive mindfulness training as a young adult and want to give to future generations, that I have written this book for you.

It's an interesting time to be a young adult. In the course of writing this book, hundreds of young adults went through my Mindfulness-Based College (MBC) program, and I connected with many of them in the process. One question I asked was, "What do you think are the biggest challenges or issues young adults are working with right now?" Examples of some of the most common answers were social media, technology, and body image. Another common response was meaninglessness, as one student said, "Honestly, I am not really for organized religion, but it kind of feels like they pulled the rug out from under society and didn't replace it with anything. Mindfulness and science have helped me make sense of the world and appreciate the beauty that is here and understand my place in it, and I am very grateful for that." Another shared, "Economics are an enormous issue for my generation. We are saddled with huge amounts of debt from our education before we even get into work. Not to mention the cost of living has gone up so substantially. There are more hurdles to achieving financial stability that then influence lifestyle stability." If you feel stressed, you are not alone.

An American Psychological Association survey showed that US adolescents' stress levels are now higher than adults for the first time since these data have been recorded (Anderson et al. 2014). Mental illnesses for young adults, including anxiety and depression, have risen steadily since the 1940s (Twenge et al. 2010; Center for Collegiate Mental Health 2021). Not to mention the rise in obesity, sedentary lifestyles, sleep problems, and addiction, all of which influence both physical and mental well-being. It's no real surprise why.

We have the same gene pool as prior generations, so clearly changes in the environment are exacerbating these issues of mental and physical ill-being. We have seen rising economic stressors, like income instability, job insecurity, the gig economy, crippling college tuition rates, and housing prices that outpace inflation, making what was possible for our parents less likely for us. There is constant encouragement in the media to eat processed food and engage in sedentary activities, like video streaming and social media. An increasing proportion of jobs are sedentary. Norms in social gatherings have changed dramatically as club and church memberships have declined in recent generations. We have become increasingly socially isolated and lonely, all while trying to connect in meaningful ways digitally. Does any of that resonate with you? If it does, you have found the right book. This book offers a scientifically tested solution to these growing problems.

Despite the challenges for young adults right now, it is also a remarkable time of opportunity. The life span of adults in the last one hundred years has doubled, so even if you are making a right mess of your life right now, you've got more time to recover than ever before. The "work from anywhere" movement is giving many people more freedom to live where and how they want. In my case, I am grateful to be currently writing in my car at a lighthouse in New England, after having gone surfing. For young adults now, it's possible to stay connected to people from around the world in nanoseconds, whether it's your friends, family, or influencers who inspire you. We have discovered neuroplasticity, where we learn and grow through our entire lives. There are technologies like mindfulness and meditation trainings that literally rewire our brains to support wise and considered change that fosters our health and happiness and even enhances performance in our areas of passion. Mindfulness can even help us realize what our areas of passion are, if we don't already know, through enhancing our self-awareness. We are building on generations of science and contemplative practice, where the determinants of health and happiness are pretty clear, and many are within our sphere of influence: diet, physical activity, sleep, social connections, and a sense of purpose, to name a few. Not only that, but we have technologies, which are presented in this book, that help us take action on whatever areas in this sphere we want, to maximize our performance, health, and happiness not only in ourselves, but also in the communities we serve.

I asked young adults who had gone through mindfulness training, "What do you see is the biggest way mindfulness could help young adults?" Travis answered, "What it will allow for young adults to do is cut through the bullshit. For example, for me, do I want to do a PhD or teach kids and make art?" It allowed Travis to realize what feels wholesome to him and what makes him happy and serves his community well. It helped him be courageous in the presence of social pressure and do what he loves and is good at, which is teaching kids and making art. Paul, on the other hand, shared, "I think it's a wonderful way to meet the good, the bad, and the ugly, and it's a way to access what is actually here. For me, mindfulness helped with my agency. If I can choose where to place my mind, overall, I become a lot better on where to place my energy. I am not consumed by material things. Even when things are bleak, there is always some choice." Sabrina shared, "You don't need to reach nirvana or enlightenment or get to the final stages of Buddhism to just be present for simple points throughout the day, like eating healthily, getting exercise, and appreciating relationships." So let's see what mindfulness actually is.

What Is Mindfulness?

Mindfulness is a present-moment awareness of our thoughts, emotions, and physical sensations, carried out with nonjudgment, gentleness, curiosity, and acceptance. It is a means to getting to know ourselves intimately through techniques that enhance self-awareness, attention control, and emotional regulation (Tang et al. 2015). Once mastered, these three self-regulation skills can be applied to all areas of life, especially those that influence well-being. We're better able to allow ourselves to be open to the subtle messages that the body, mind, heart, and spirit are sending us.

An element of mindfulness is *remembrance* or *bringing to mind* (Gethin 2015). I recently came across a description by Buddhadāsa Bhikkhu (1987), who described how the Pāli word for mindfulness (*sati*) shares the same root as the Pāli word for arrow (*sara*). Like an arrow, mindfulness is seen as being fast, in that it brings to mind our wisdom in this moment. Can we be right here, right now, with a conduit to our wisdom within, so we can respond skillfully to anything that arises?

I remember my mindfulness teacher Joanne Friday shared that when people asked her what she did for a living, she replied that her career was to respond skillfully to life. Sometimes responding skillfully means to move toward uncomfortable feelings and sensations rather than away, while respecting our emotional and physical limits. While it can be challenging, approaching is often easier than expected, and doing so allows us to see the root of challenges more clearly, leading to valuable and accurate insight or a fuller picture of reality. Compared to the often-used technique of avoiding challenging emotions, thoughts, or physical sensations, we become like the scientist who looks at all the data to see the truth, as opposed to only looking for what we want to see. In turn, we craft a wiser path forward to help us succeed, boost our well-being, and build the life we want.

The better we get at being mindful, the more fluid life becomes, and the better we become at responding skillfully to each moment. It becomes easier for us to choose healthy coping strategies in the moment, such as taking a break and having a cup of tea outside under a tree, rather than demolishing a bag of chocolate chip cookies. It can also allow for faster recovery from stressors when they arise, as they inevitably do for all of us. When practiced regularly, mindfulness gives us the capacity to improve our health in the whole sense, which is defined by the World Health Organization as "a state of complete physical, mental, and social well-being and not merely the absence of disease or infirmity" (World Health Organization 1948).

In this book, I weave four elements throughout every chapter: science, mindfulness practices, stories from young adults who have gone through mindfulness training, and the notion of health and happiness. I also invite you to work through two major phases that will change your life.

In the first phase, there is an opportunity to learn about the wisdom of the body (chapter 1), heart (chapter 2), mind (chapter 3), and spirit (chapter 4), as well as practices for opening up to this wisdom. You can discover ways to gently and respectfully acknowledge what is present for you in your body (physical sensations), heart (emotions), mind (thoughts, consciousness), and spirit (nature of reality). These four domains are arguably the entirety of the human experience. Just as a skilled bicycle mechanic deeply knows every part of a bicycle and how to set it up for maximum performance, when we open these domains, we know ourselves and what we need to do to be happier and healthier, which are among the deepest of natural desires. By coupling this self-awareness with meditation training that improves attention control, we can direct our enhanced attention to take action on the messages that the body, heart, mind, and spirit are giving us.

This book leverages a system developed about twenty-five hundred years ago by the Buddha that involves sixteen contemplations in the Discourse on Breathing Mindfulness (Shaw 2006). This discourse is among the oldest Buddhist teachings and is known in the ancient language Pāli as the *Ānāpānsati Sutta*. The word "ānāpānsati" is quite broad in its meaning and has been translated as "to recall anything at all with mindfulness while breathing in and out" (Buddhadāsa Bikkhu 1988). The Buddha himself declared that he realized self-awakening through the practice of ānāpānsati (Buddhadāsa Bikkhu 1988). Zen master, scholar, and peace activist Thich Nhat Hanh shared that, "I was so happy on the day I found this sutra. I thought I'd discovered the greatest treasure on earth" (Nhat Hanh 2008).

I have been personally working with it for about twenty years, and there are few if any teachings that have brought me more happiness, health, and wisdom. The discourse is divided into four sections, each with four contemplations. In many ways, the first four are on using mindfulness and the breath to open the body (chapter 1), the second four to open the heart (emotions, chapter 2), the third four to open the mind (mental formations such as thoughts, chapter 3), and the last four to open the spirit (to clearly see the reality of nature or truth, chapter 4). You can also find all sixteen contemplations in the discourse in appendix 2.

I adapted the Discourse for this book and added relevant teachings. I relied primarily on four translations, from Pāli or Chinese, by three authors—a Buddhist scholar at Oxford University, a Vietnamese Zen master, and a Thai Buddhist monk and teacher—each with unique commentaries (Buddhadāsa Bhikkhu 1988; Shaw 2006; Nhat Hanh 2008).

While these contemplations have roots in Buddhism, it is not my intention to convert you to that religion. Indeed, I encourage you to keep your spiritual roots, whatever they are, and not to cut yourself off at your roots. The Buddha himself didn't consider his teachings to be a religion; they are just some contemplations that often lead to improved happiness and health and are offered in that light. They can be woven into any religious or spiritual faith (or lack thereof) in ways that are respectful to that wisdom tradition.

While the Discourse on Breathing Mindfulness is used as an organizing structure, this book is not designed to be a commentary on the Discourse. There are other good books focused on that (Shaw 2006; Nhat Hanh 2008; Buddhadāsa Bhikkhu 1988; Anālayo 2019; Rosenberg 1998). This book is designed to provide you with mindfulness training that is influenced in part by the Discourse along with the clinical research in young adults, so you can develop evidence-informed skills to help you succeed, boost your well-being, and build the life you want.

In the second phase (chapters 5 and 6), I will guide you in applying that wisdom to this moment—not just during blissful moments when you're sitting on a cushion and meditating, but during very practical scenarios including your career path, life's path, performance in your areas of interest (arts, athletics, academics, and so forth), social media and screen use, along with your relationship to the social environment (friends, family, romantic partners, work or school colleagues), political environment, and physical environment (particularly your home and natural environment). Recordings of the guided meditations can be found on the website for this book, http://www.newharbinger.com/49135.

Research in the field of mindfulness neuroscience has shown that, when practiced regularly, mindfulness changes our brain physiology, making us more aware and helping us use the different regions of the brain more skillfully (Gotink et al. 2016; Tang et al. 2015). While many of us are daunted by the idea of "enlightenment" or "awakening," viewing them as if they were something to attain in another lifetime, I will present them—along with other lofty concepts such as wisdom, nonjudgment, joy, and flourishing—as if they were your birthright. Because they are.

Chapter 7 takes mindfulness a step further by nudging you to ask questions that lead to insights to help you match your skills and interests with the greatest needs of society and the planet. In this way, you can be completely self-expressed, doing important work.

Mindfulness is not a cure-all. Throughout the book, I encourage critical thinking by bringing up some of the current controversies associated with mindfulness, including the following questions: Can mindfulness-based programs cause adverse events, such as panic attacks and psychotic breaks? Can mindfulness just dull us to be more accepting of atrocities to human, social, and environmental rights? By stepping toward controversies with openness and curiosity, rather than stepping away, we can allow truth and insight to arise.

Mindfulness-Based College and Young Adults

My Mindfulness-Based College (MBC) program began in 2015 at the behest of Brown University students who were suffering from the challenges facing emerging adults. Initially, I developed a for-credit course called Meditation, Mindfulness, and Health, which has become very popular at Brown and has been shown to reduce students' stress.

Based on the early findings and the needs of young adults, I developed MBC as a noncredit program for all young adults regardless of where they live or whether they are in college. MBC is grounded in the evidence-based Jon Kabat-Zinn's (2013) Mindfulness-Based Stress Reduction (MBSR) program, which has undergone hundreds of randomized controlled trials (de Vibe et al. 2017). As a certified MBSR instructor, I developed MBC specifically for young adults and their priorities (Loucks et al. 2021). Scientific findings suggest that MBC changes lives. For example, a randomized controlled trial by my team showed that MBC significantly improved overall health, depressive symptoms, sleep quality, sedentary activity, and loneliness in students who took the program compared to the control group (Loucks et al. 2021).

While this book is geared toward young adults, all generations of readers can benefit from it, especially those looking to improve health, well-being, and performance using an evidence-informed approach.

Taking Stock and Looking Ahead

Mindfulness, I believe, has a place in everyone's life if it is learned in skill-ful ways. It's accessible at any time, day or night, and the practical applications are endless. The practice helps us stay focused on what is important now, even when it is challenging, and to have the self-awareness to know when and how to care for our body, heart, mind, and spirit while also caring for our family, society, and the environment. In many ways, mindfulness can be applied to any aspect of life.

Knowing what you want to focus on in this book and this program will make it relevant to you and allow you to get the most out of it. Also, in the future, as you have different elements to work on, you may find yourself rereading the book with that new area you want to develop in mind.

Self-Reflection Exercise: Assess Your Baseline Well-Being

The intention of this exercise is to assess your baseline well-being now, to take a step back and see where you are and where you want to go. At the end of this book, you will be invited to answer these questions again to see what changed, if anything. So I encourage you to reflect on these questions and jot the answers down so you can find them again when you are finishing the book.

1. How many servings of vegetables do you typically eat in a day? A serving size is ½ cup.[1]

2. How many servings of fruits do you typically eat in a day? A serving size is ½ cup of fresh fruit or a ¼ cup of dried fruit.[2]

3. How much physical activity do you get in a typical day (everywhere such as at work, school, and home)?[3]

   a. Vigorous physical activity includes things like carrying heavy loads, digging, playing soccer, or bicycling quickly (answer in hours or minutes).

b.   Moderate physical activity includes things like carrying light loads, bicycling at a regular pace, mowing the lawn, or brisk walking (answer in hours or minutes).

4.   How much screen time (smartphone, tablet, gaming, computer, television) in a typical day do you engage in where it is the primary activity (not counting if you have it on in the background when doing another activity, like exercising). Note that many smartphones and tablets measure this.[4]

5.   How many hours of actual sleep do you typically get at night? (This is probably different than the number of hours you are in bed.)[5]

6.   How stressed do you feel? For example, in the last month, how often have you felt difficulties were piling up so high that you could not overcome them?[6] The answer options are (a) never, (b) almost never, (c) sometimes; (d) fairly often, or (e) very often.

7.   In the past month, how often have you used the following, where the answer options are (a) never, (b) once or twice, (c) weekly, or (d) daily or almost daily?[7]

Binge-drinking alcohol (which is five or more drinks a day for men, and four or more drinks a day for women)

Tobacco products (vaping, cigarettes, chewing tobacco)

Other mood-altering drugs for nonmedical reasons

8.   Now let's shift gears a little. I invite you to identify your areas of focus and passion. Maybe it's a particular area of study, type of work, or relationship with a loved one. Maybe it is a sport or a musical instrument. What are your areas of focus or passion that you want to explore? I invite you to name two.

Area 1 (name it).

How does your performance in this area of focus match with what you feel your innate potential is? Answer options are (a) much lower, (b) moderately lower, (c) slightly lower, or (d) matches my potential.

Area 2 (name it).

How does your performance in this area of focus match with what you feel your innate potential is? Answer options are (a) much lower, (b) moderately lower, (c) slightly lower, or (d) matches my potential.

9. What else do you feel significantly affects your health and happiness that hasn't been named in the above questions (such as social relationships, time in nature, and so forth)?

Domain 1 (name it).

How does your level in this domain compare to what you feel is ideal? Answer options are (a) very different than ideal level, (b) moderately different than ideal level, (c) slightly different from ideal level, or (d) ideal level.

Domain 2 (name it).

How does your level in this domain compare to what you feel is ideal? Answer options are (a) very different than ideal level, (b) moderately different than ideal level, (c) slightly different from ideal level, or (d) ideal level.

This self-reflection will allow you to take a step back and reflect on what you want to focus on at this time in your life and the work you want to do as you read this book. The recommended levels of these factors are shown in appendix 1 in case you would like to see how you compare to experts' advice.

Now, I invite you to look over your answers to all the questions above and self-reflect on how pleased you are with how you are doing in these domains. Ask yourself, *What are the one or two main things that are limiting my health and happiness that I have control over to change and that I feel in my heart and mind that I would like to focus on while reading this book?* In other words: Why are you here? What do you really want?

In the rest of this book, we will explore how to make that happen. This book is designed to be about a seven- to fourteen-week program, with you spending a week or two on each chapter, possibly during a school term if you are a student. You don't have to do it this way of course. With mindfulness training, it is exactly that—training. The practices offered in the book, if done regularly, have the capacity to change your body and mind in healthy ways.

I look forward to helping you gain essential skills to boost your well-being and build the life you want. I'm not here with you, but then again, I am. I've written this book with you in mind. We are in relationship during the process of you reading this book. Everything is interconnected. Consequently, how this book influences you may well influence me in some way or form one day. I hope it serves you well. Let's begin.

CHAPTER 1

Opening the Body
Physical Thriving

Sabrina, a student in the Meditation, Mindfulness, and Health course, shared, "Since the end of high school, I have dealt with some eating disorders. Once quarantine happened, I started meditating. I had just returned from Australia, my nutrition had gone downhill, and my mental health was struggling. When I came home, I started meditating. It quickly became a daily routine. Before, I just exercised for body image and to burn calories. Once I became more mindful, I began to notice myself wanting to exercise because it genuinely made me feel good. I used to listen to music or, if on a treadmill, I'd watch TV—anything I could do to distract myself. Now I just focus on my body and breath. I run longer, and it's more enjoyable. I always hear people say, 'Exercise clears my head and puts me in a good mood.' Now I really feel that. Also, now instead of eating for physical body image, I find myself eating more healthy food because I feel better afterward. I feel cleaner and higher energy. Mindfulness helped me feel better for my health. If I stop meditating, I can quickly fall into bad habits of the past. Now meditation has become a requirement in my life."

We live in a time of digital media and advertising telling us we will be happy if we eat certain things and look a certain way. Most of us have sedentary jobs that don't provide much physical activity, not to mention most of us commute to work in sedentary ways and have sedentary pastimes. It's pretty easy to get substances that give us an altered state, whether it's alcohol, cannabis, sugar, or caffeinated energy drinks. This is neat in many ways, and it is creating the most obese, out of shape, addicted, mentally ill society, possibly in history. If you struggle with your diet, physical activity, addiction, stress, anxiety, or sleep, you are not alone. And in fact, it's not really your fault. Our genomes haven't mutated fast enough for the increases in obesity, sedentary activity, and sleep problems to be genetically driven, so it must be our environment and our genes interacting with that environment.

Tapping into the body by giving it your attention and awareness is one way to address those health-diminishing issues—or to prevent them from happening in the first place. The body is a remarkable organism. It's capable of telling you what it needs—via feelings, sensations, aches, pains, and even thoughts. When you tap into the body, you're going straight to the source for the most accurate information. In doing so, it can bring you to new heights of well-being and performance that you didn't even know you could reach.

Although I didn't realize it at the time, one of my gateways into mindfulness practice began as a teenager, before I even knew what mindfulness was. When I was in high school in Victoria, British Columbia, I routinely raced in Olympic-distance triathlons, which involved a combination of swimming, biking, and running for 32 miles, or 51.5 kilometers. During these challenging races, I monitored my thoughts and body in an effort to maximize performance. If I started breathing too hard, for instance, and felt my muscles burning unnecessarily, I would note that I had moved into the anaerobic zone and pull back on my pace.

My triathlon experiences also taught me how closely the body and mind are connected. When my mind had drifted off, I'd notice I was going too slowly, and I'd increase my pace. But the opposite could happen as well. Once, during the biking stage of a race, my mind wandered to thoughts of my girlfriend and a guy who had been making unwanted advances toward her. Suddenly, I found myself hammering up a hill, ready to punch him. Then I realized it was just a thought. More important to the race, that thought was needlessly tiring me out (although, I made a mental note to look into the situation later).

Part of awakening to your full potential is awakening the body—becoming aware of its sometimes-subtle sensations and cues, as well as the overt aches and pains, by giving it focused attention and considering what it has to tell you. Listening and then responding to the body's messages not only improves performance but can prevent injury and promote healing and overall health. Your body sends you important messages about what it needs (or doesn't need) all the time. This chapter will show you how to tap into the body, listen to the messages it shares, and respond skillfully to those messages to help you succeed, boost your well-being, and build the life you want.

This chapter is organized around the first four contemplations in the Discourse on Breathing Mindfulness. These contemplations focus primarily on developing your ability to control your attention (develop concentration) by bringing awareness to an object of meditation, such as the breath, and fostering self-awareness and self-care, particularly of the body. The first four contemplations are shown below, and then in the following sections, we will explore each more deeply. All sixteen contemplations are listed in appendix 2.

DISCOURSE ON BREATHING MINDFULNESS:
First Tetrad of Contemplations

1. Breathing in, I know I am breathing in. Breathing out, I know I am breathing out.

2. Breathing in a long breath or a short breath, I know whether it is a long breath or a short breath. Breathing out a long breath or a short breath, I know whether it is a long breath or a short breath.

3. Breathing in, I am aware of my whole body. Breathing out, I am aware of my whole body.

4. Breathing in, I calm my body. Breathing out, I calm my body.

Anchoring the Mind to the Body

There are two ways to categorize meditation training: one is focused attention, and the other is open monitoring. This translates into attention-control training (focused attention) and self-awareness training (open monitoring)—two of the major mechanisms by which MBC and other programs are proposed to improve well-being—as shown in figure 1.1 below. In most meditation traditions, and increasingly in the science, when we begin to train our mind, we start with focused-attention training. There is evidence that this approach reduces stress (Cullen et al. 2021).

Evidence also shows (Loucks et al. 2019; Loucks et al. 2021; Tang et al. 2015) that mindfulness and meditation can help improve our ability to self-regulate, as shown in the grey box in figure 1.1, with a particular focus on training our self-awareness (awareness of our physical sensations, emotions, and thoughts), attention control (our ability to place our mind where we want to), and emotional regulation. We can then apply these self-regulation skills to our relationship with the factors that most influence our well-being, such as those shown in the bottom box of figure 1.1, like diet, physical activity, social relationships, or even our relationship with digital media.

The self-reflection questions in the introduction were designed to help you pick the factors (shown in the bottom box) you want to focus on while reading this book. But in the mindfulness training path, it is usually recommended to start with training on focused attention (Cullen et al. 2021), with some emphasis on self-awareness as well, such as meditating on the breath. These are the first two steps in the Discourse on Breathing Mindfulness.

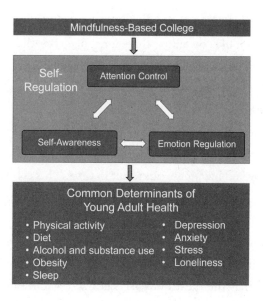

Figure 1.1 Theoretical framework for how Mindfulness-Based College is expected to influence young adults' well-being and performance.

DISCOURSE ON BREATHING MINDFULNESS:

First Two Contemplations

1. *Breathing in, I know I am breathing in. Breathing out, I know I am breathing out.*

2. *Breathing in a long breath or a short breath, I know whether it is a long breath or a short breath. Breathing out a long breath or a short breath, I know whether it is a long breath or a short breath.*

These contemplations offer basic training in attention control, placing your attention where you want to place it, in this case on the breath, and self-awareness, being aware of the breath, including how the mind and body feel when the breath is long or short. Physiologically, the lungs and brain are connected to each other in part via the vagus nerve, which is activated with long breaths. Activation of the vagus nerve has been shown to positively influence mood, in part through parasympathetic nervous system activity, which has calming properties (Gerritsen and Band 2018). Try it now if you like, by taking three long, deep breaths.

Note that, in this contemplation and in general, a long breath isn't necessarily better than a short breath. We are just coming to know ourselves a little better right now, including the characteristics of the breath, such as how deep, shallow, fast, slow, long, or short it is, and how that type of breath makes us feel. In doing so, concentration arrives, self-awareness grows, and joy and happiness can result in time. This contemplation is an avenue into mindful awareness, focusing first on the breath, if that is a comfortable place for you to focus on.

Mindfulness science is starting to show that not everyone is comfortable with their breath as an anchor point. For example, some people have asthma such that the breath doesn't feel like a calm, safe place. At the Mindfulness Center at Brown University, as several other mindfulness-based program providers have done, we introduce other anchor points, such as the palms of the hands, soles of the feet, or even sound (Treleaven 2018). Another recommended anchor point is an inch or two below the naval (belly button), which in many ways is the central location in the body. The important thing is to find an anchor point that will always be with you and that you are comfortable using as an object of meditation.

While the breath has benefit in that it is always changing and it connects the head to the body—as the air flows in through the mouth and nose and into the body (chest) and then circulates through the body—another part of the body or sound can be a good anchor too. But if the breath is comfortable for you, I invite you to use it as there is more research available showing benefits of meditation on the breath.

After the anchor point, the next part of meditation is the setup of your body. This has to do with posture, and there are priorities: comfort and alertness. If you picture someone meditating, they might be sitting on a cushion cross-legged. That is personally my favorite position, but you don't need to use it. I value the concept of nonviolence, including toward ourselves. So if that position is painful for you, choose one that is "not violent" for you. When we can have some comfort in our meditation

posture, it is more conducive to focusing the mind where it is most productive to be in this moment, instead of focusing on the discomfort in our
legs, for example. However, if we maximize *comfort* too much (such as
lying in bed with a soft pillow), it might affect the other element to priori-
tize, which is *alertness*. The reason I like sitting cross-legged is that it has
become fairly comfortable and it promotes alertness (because my core
muscles need to be engaged so I don't fall over). However, find what is
best for you. Try kneeling or sitting on a chair, with your spine upright
and away from the back of the chair. We each have different bodies and
presence or absence of pain, so I invite you to find a posture that maximizes comfort and alertness for you today.

The next piece is what to do with the eyes. I recommend having them
closed most of the way so you cut out the visual field, allowing you to turn
inward with less distraction. However, you might like to keep the eyelids
slightly open to allow light to come through and activate the photorecep-
tors in the eyes, thereby fostering alertness.

Okay, let's try it now. (You can find an audio recording of this and the
other meditations on the website for this book, http://www.newharbinger.
com/49135, and in the free downloadable Mindfulness-Based College app.)

Focused-Attention Meditation

The main intention of this meditation is to train the mind to be where we want
it to be, in this case, on an object of meditation, such as the breath, a part of
the body, or sound. If you are comfortable using the breath as the object of
meditation, I encourage that. If another part of the body, such as the palms of
the hands or soles of the feet, or even sound feels safer, that is fine too. The
point is to find an object of meditation that is with you every moment of the
day. This object can become your "anchor point" to keep you grounded when
you need it and a tool to help you to develop your ability to place your mind
where you want to.

Each time you notice the mind has wandered, which in many ways is a
moment of mindfulness, come back to the present. In those moments, just

notice with qualities of curiosity and nonjudgment where the mind is dwelling, as that is good information about how and who you are today. For example, did the mind go to the future or the past? Does it usually go to the future or usually go to the past? Did it go somewhere familiar where it often dwells, or did it go somewhere new? It's not "good" or "bad" where the mind went or even that it went somewhere at all. It's just information. And then, invite the mind back, with both gentleness and firmness, to the object of meditation.

Through this process, we develop both attention control, by training ourselves to concentrate on an object of our choosing, and self-awareness, by coming to know our sensations, emotions, and thoughts as the mind drifts toward them—all in the context of the mindfulness qualities of curiosity, gentleness, nonjudgment, and nonstriving. (Nonstriving refers to not grasping for something to be different in the future in a way that brings us away from the present moment.)

This is a strong combination of training that can help us self-regulate, thereby harnessing our bodies and minds at their full capacity and building the life we want. For many experienced meditators, if they had to pick one meditation to practice for a lifetime, this would probably be it, given how fundamental it is and that it can lead to strong development of attention control, self-awareness, curiosity, nonstriving, insight, and wisdom.

Settling into a posture that will support your comfort and alertness for meditation.

Taking a moment to find your way to your anchor point. For most, this will be the breath. If the breath isn't a place of safety or comfort for you, you are welcome to use an alternate anchor, like a part of the body, such as the palms of the hands or the soles of the feet, or even sound if you prefer.

If your anchor point is the breath: Inviting you connect with it—with the in-breath and out-breath. Allowing thoughts to settle so all you are doing is being right here with this object of meditation—the breath. Noticing the sensations of the breath where it is first coming in and last leaving the body, such as at the tip of the nose. Aware of the breath flowing in, pausing as it changes direction, flowing out, pausing, and so on.

If your anchor point is a part of the body: Bringing awareness to the sensations of touch, lack of touch, warmth, or coolness.

If your anchor point is sound: Seeing if you can be there with the raw elements of sound, like pitch, how rhythmic or arrhythmic the sound is, or volume. Any time you give meaning to the sound (for example, that is a truck going by, a bird song, or a clock) just letting go of giving it meaning and returning to the raw elements of that sound, like its pitch, rhythm, or volume.

For all anchor points: Each time the mind wanders away from the object of meditation, noticing where it went with kindness and without judgment. That's good information about how we are today and who we are. Inviting the mind back to the object of the meditation: to the breath, the body, or sound.

If your anchor point is the breath: Aware of the speed of breath, noticing how long or short the breath is, how deep or shallow. Recognizing there is no "right" length or depth of the breath, just coming to know it a little better right now.

If your anchor point is a part of the body: Perhaps noticing moisture or dryness, movement, lack of movement, touch, or lack of touch in the region of the body that is your anchor point.

If your anchor point is sound: Noticing whether each sound is inside or outside the room if you are in a room or how close or far away each sound is if you are in an open space. Recognizing that the soundscape is like a story unfolding as different sounds arise and fade away. Can you be there moment by moment for the unfolding story of sound?

For all anchor points: Seeing if you can allow thoughts to settle out, kind of like how mud settles in stirred-up water when the water becomes still so all that is left is the object of meditation, like the breath, the body, or sound.

As the meditation comes to a close, inviting you to bring this concentration to the next step in your day or evening, being fully there with the next priority that you are engaging with.

Listening to the Body

My student Brady shared that he developed ulcerative colitis as a teenager. He described the disease as mostly genetically caused, but for those who get it in their teenage years, it usually has something to do with stress or anxiety. Brady said, "I think the stress I was under in high school accelerated it. When I developed it, it made me think about what I was doing that led to that. I realized I wasn't taking care of myself—through exercise, sleep, social outlets." Once Brady started taking his disease more seriously in college and thinking about himself with kindness, it helped him change. He now eats more vegetables, fish, and chicken and less fatty substances, and gets more rest. Brady shared that, "I think the most important thing that has impacted my condition is sleep. Going to bed at a reasonable time and waking at a reasonable time." Brady shared that he was developing more control over his mind, so instead of his mind racing while trying to move toward sleep, it was now quieter and more focused. In fact, he has stopped taking melatonin to help him sleep. Part of what mindfulness training brought to Brady was greater awareness of his body, and how by working with his mind (such as by letting racing thoughts go while drifting off to sleep), he could in turn care for his body. This brings us to the third contemplation in the Discourse on Breathing Mindfulness:

DISCOURSE ON BREATHING MINDFULNESS:
Third Contemplation

3. *Breathing in, I am aware of my whole body. Breathing out, I am aware of my whole body.*

My understanding of the "breathing in..." and "breathing out..." elements—of all sixteen contemplations in the Discourse on Breathing Mindfulness—is that they are offered as a way for us to stay grounded while we engage in each contemplation, such as in this case with awareness of the body. With all the contemplations in this discourse, if the breath is not a safe place for you, you are welcome to replace the words "breathing in... breathing out..." with the words "staying connected to my anchor point (a specific part of the body or sound)...," if that feels better for your well-being.

Similarly, if there are parts of the body that do not feel safe to bring mindful awareness to at this time (recognizing this may shift over time, but doesn't need to), you are welcome to replace the contemplation "I am aware of my whole body" with "I am aware of physical sensations," letting the physical sensations in areas of the body you feel safe with to become the objects of meditation, as you come to know these parts of the body just a little better in this moment.

One of the key concepts introduced in Mindfulness-Based Stress Reduction (MBSR) and MBC is the triangle of awareness, shown in figure 1.2. The three parts of the triangle are the three components of self-awareness: (1) physical sensations, (2) emotions, and (3) thoughts, which in many ways make up the entire human experience. Can you think of any experience that isn't in one of those three domains?

We often clump awareness of these three domains into one messy sense of general self-awareness. In doing so, it can be challenging to understand and parse out where to efficiently intervene—for example, maybe just on relieving a particular physical pain or a specific emotion or thought—to improve how we feel. Throughout this book, you will spend time developing your self-awareness of each, but in this chapter, we are focusing on physical sensations. You can use the triangle of awareness as a tool to be self-aware, pause, and skillfully respond to stressors, which we'll discuss further in future chapters. For now, we're going concentrate on further developing our awareness of the body and befriending it—this partner in life.

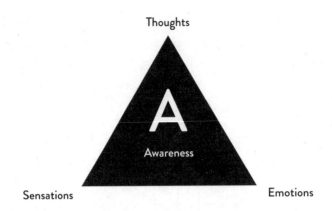

Figure 1.2   The triangle of awareness: (1) physical sensations, (2) emotions, and (3) thoughts. In many ways, the entire human experience is in these three domains.

The first way we train awareness of physical sensations is with the body scan. This is a self-awareness practice, which involves connecting with the body while at the same time fostering attention control by training the mind to be there with each part of the body in a gentle, nonjudgmental, curious way. Body scan meditation recordings of varying lengths are available on the MBC app and the website for this book, http://www.newharbinger.com/49135.

The Body Scan Meditation

The intention of the body scan meditation is to focus curious, nonjudgmental attention on each and every part of the body to see what messages, or lack of messages, are there. It is an opportunity to spend time with, and get to know, the body a little more, and see how each region is in this moment of your life. From this awareness, it can create opportunities for insights to arise on how to care for, and harness, your body to help you succeed, boost well-being, and build the life you want.

While bringing nonjudgmental curious awareness to each part of the body, I encourage you to respect your limits. For example, if there is a part of the body that has experienced a difficult event and it is overwhelming to connect with, you can offer kindness and compassion to yourself and either come back to your anchor point (the breath, a different part of the body, or sound) or skip that part of the body. I encourage you to stay in your comfort zone or a zone that, while not entirely comfortable, offers you growth. If this practice is too much for you right now, you can also let it go, and if at another time in the future, it resonates with you, you might like to explore it then.

Inviting you to find a quiet place, away from noise and distraction, if possible.

If you can lie down, that's ideal, although sitting is okay if you prefer.

Taking a moment to check in with an anchor point, such as the breath, to allow your attention to focus within. You are encouraged to do this for a minute or two, to allow your attention to settle into this moment, this anchor point of the breath, body, or sound.

Noticing the sensations of the body where it makes contact what you are resting on, whether a chair, couch, or bed.

Noticing that physical feeling, say, of touch or pressure.

Beginning to scan through your body slowly, starting with the left big toe. Noticing what sensations are here, such as touch or lack of touch, warmth, coolness, moisture. Offering curiosity to what is being sensed in this part of the body in this moment.

Slowly bringing awareness in turn through the left foot, ankle, lower leg, knee, thigh, and hip.

Holding the entire left leg in awareness and noticing how it feels now, compared to when you started checking in with it.

Next, shifting to the right big toe and so on, guiding your awareness to each and every part of the body, letting the body be just as it is—not needing to change it in any way but coming to understand it and how it is in this moment.

As you check in with your body, noticing which sensations are there, such as warmth, coolness, a breeze on the skin, a pain, an area that is feeling good, and so on.

Do those sensations remain steady, or do they shift and change moment to moment?

Continuing this scan through the rest of your body, such as the torso, back muscles, shoulders, arms, hands, fingers, neck, mouth, nose, eyes, ears, and brain. Allowing, even just for this moment, each and every part of your body to be just as it is.

Noticing if there are parts that you wish were different, and for this moment, letting those wishes go and allowing the body to be just as it is. As Jon Kabat-Zinn (2013), the creator of MBSR, has shared, as long as you are breathing, there is more right with you than wrong with you, no matter what is wrong. Can you be with each and every part of the body, just as it is, opening to the messages that it is sharing?

As the body scan comes toward an end, enveloping the entire body in awareness. Noticing what arises in the sensations of the body. For example, are certain areas communicating more strongly than others in this moment?

Seeing if you can be here for it all, while respecting your limits, and coming to know your body just a little better.

Mindfulness can allow you to know and befriend your body in ways you never imagined. For example, think of a time when you went on trip with a group of people. Maybe it was a road trip or vacation with friends or family where you spent a lot of time together. How did you feel toward most of your fellow travelers when you returned? Did you feel closer? Did you care more about them? With meditation and mindfulness, we begin to spend more time with ourselves in a kind, gentle, curious, accepting way. Through that process, we often come to understand ourselves better and want to care for ourselves more. In the paragraphs below, you will have an opportunity to explore how to come to know your body better, and care for it, so it can become as healthy and happy as possible.

The second major approach to bring awareness to the body while staying anchored is mindful movement, specifically yoga. Note that there are many forms of mindful movement, such as tai chi, qi gong, and others. Here we use yoga, but others may be similarly or uniquely effective for you.

Movement can complement the body scan because, through movement, our body may tell us things we need to know that it wouldn't as easily share when we are motionless in a body scan. At your next opportunity, stretch every muscle and tendon in your body and see what they share with you. Can you be there with the messages—with curiosity, acceptance, and without judgment? See what arises, knowing that it occurred for some reason, whether genetic, environmental (such as studying for long hours, working a sedentary desk job, or the consequence of a car accident), or otherwise.

With mindfulness, you can bring awareness to that experience and also to the cause of the experience. Armed with that information, you can consider the skillful next step to bring you forward in fruitful ways. Example yoga poses are shown in videos on the website for this book, http://www.newharbinger.com/49135. The yoga poses offered there have been particularly helpful for people who find that moving their body allows them to better come into the moment and let distractions go.

Caring for the Body

The fourth contemplation in the Discourse on Breathing Mindfulness can help you leverage your attention control based on what you learned through the practices that fostered self-awareness and attention control, such as the focused-attention meditation, body scan, and yoga.

DISCOURSE ON BREATHING MINDFULNESS:
Fourth Contemplation

4. *Breathing in, I calm my body. Breathing out, I calm my body.*

I tend to adapt this one as: "Breathing in, I calm my body. Breathing out, I care for my body."

This contemplation can offer calming opportunities for the body, which can happen through concentration on the breath or other object of meditation. When we are fully concentrated on an object (the breath, the body, even writing a term paper, or engaged in a sport or artistic expression), there can be a calm to it, as we are in the zone, fully there with what we are focusing on. By being with the body, as in the third contemplation ("I am aware of my whole body…"), the body can offer messages, and through the fourth contemplation, we can be working to not only calm the body, but also care for it, including identifying the highest-priority ways it would be best cared for.

In fact, this book, while anchored around the Discourse on Breathing Mindfulness, has a few unique messages that are somewhat distinct from the Discourse, or at least from the translations I have accessed. One is the explicit emphasis on caring for the body. In many ways this contemplation, as I adapted it, is about expanding your attention control and self-awareness to listen to what your body needs and wants, and then placing your attention on offering it that, which can then bring health and happiness. This sets the stage for us to make health-supporting choices.

Certain low-hanging fruits are fundamental to good physical health. I won't dwell on them, as I suspect you know that physical activity, diet, sleep, and limiting alcohol and other drugs influence physical and mental well-being. I boiled down the basics here for you. If some of these areas could use some improvement for you (as they could for most of us, including me), they may be places to consider focusing on, as they provide big returns on investment.

A Healthy Diet

My favorite quote about diet is author Michael Pollan's (2007), "Eat food. Not too much. Mostly plants. That, more or less, is the short answer to the supposedly incredibly complicated and confusing question of what we humans should eat in order to be· maximally healthy." In parallel, former First Lady Michelle Obama worked with the USDA to create MyPlate: the idea is to fill each meal with about half fruits and vegetables. In diet research, fads come and go, but I have never seen anyone quibble about the value of vegetables. Evidence-based plans, such as the Mediterranean and the DASH (Dietary Approaches to Stop Hypertension) diets (Sotos-Prieto et al. 2017), generally emphasize high consumption of vegetables, fruits, whole grains, beans, nuts, and seeds. They encourage healthy fats, such as olive oil. Dairy products, fish, and poultry are consumed in low to moderate amounts.

However, we are also nonjudgmental about it. Instead, what's important is the kind of diet feels best to *your* body. Being omnivores, we humans can digest a remarkable variety of foods, and we also each possess differences, such as gluten or lactose intolerances. I invite you to mindfully explore which diet feels best to your body while aiming for about half of what you eat to be fruits and vegetables.

Mindful Eating Meditation

The intention of this meditation is to create conditions to support a deepening understanding of how specific foods affect you by eating an emotionally laden snack—such as something sweet, salty, or even healthy. I invite you to find a tasty snack high in sugar or salt, such as a muffin, cookie, or chips. Choose one of your favorite foods that is probably not very healthy for you and triggers a fairly strong emotion-like craving. Alternatively, pick something that is healthy and triggers strong emotions (positive or negative). If you aren't grabbing the snack now, then call it to mind.

Through this mindfulness exercise, I encourage you to explore your limits but not go beyond them. For example, if you struggle with binge-eating, I'd recommend you tread lightly around selecting an item. Pick something that will explore limits but is unlikely to trigger a binge. If you have an aversion to foods, offer lots of self-kindness and even skip this exercise if you feel that bringing more awareness to your relationship with eating a specific food is not healthy for you in this moment. Okay, let's begin.

Noticing what is happening in your physical sensations as you read this or have the food item in front of you. Is anything there? Such as a watering mouth? A surge of energy to get up and grab that bag of chips? What about in the domain of emotions and thoughts?

Here you are, in a safe environment with no one looking, coming to know yourself perhaps just a little bit better and how you are around sweet, salty, or healthy foods, or at least this particular food. You're coming to know yourself in a nonjudgmental, curious way.

Now I invite you—while keeping in mind the triangle of awareness of physical sensations, thoughts, and emotions (figure 1.2)—to be there with the food you've selected visually. Right now, you are just looking at it.

What arises in your physical sensations, emotions, and thoughts now, in this moment?

As you continue to slowly explore the food item through the sensations of touch, what are you noticing as you move it around with your finger, exploring how it feels?

Bringing this food item up to your nose and noticing the smell. What is experienced in the sensations, emotions, and thoughts as you bring the sense of smell to this food item?

And now bringing the item to touch your lip, but not yet putting it in your mouth.

Then, as you are ready, placing it on the tongue but not yet biting it. What is sensed here as it rests on the tongue? Noticing with the mindfulness quality of curiosity and nonjudgment.

Then, inviting you to take one bite, but just one. What arises as you take that single bite?

Now as you are ready, beginning to chew the item, aware of the sensations as each chew transpires. Aware of the desire to swallow, and when the times comes, inviting you to swallow with the conscious decision to do so rather than unconsciously doing so.

Taking a moment to connect in with the sensations, emotions, and thoughts now that the food item has been swallowed. What is here?

Then inviting you to engage in this way to what is left of the food item, recognizing when the desire comes up to stop eating, and respecting that desire.

Noticing how your body and mind feel. Many of us are affected both positively and negatively by particular foods. How did this particular food item affect you, if it did?

Knowing that this present moment is influenced by prior moments, inviting you to notice how the moment was affected by what you did and didn't eat. Exploring this with gentleness and caring for yourself and seeing if any insights arise around skillful next steps.

As the meditation comes to a close, inviting you to set an alarm for twenty minutes or even an hour, or take note of the time, and check in with yourself about the how food you just ate affects your mood, body, and thoughts in the longer term.

This moment is influenced by prior moments, including what you may have eaten, drank, or smoked, and how you physically exercised. The contemplation exercise can increase your awareness about how what you eat affects you. How is this moment influenced by what you last ate? How is this moment influenced by what you usually eat?

A participant who went through one of our mindfulness programs shared, "I've given myself time to go outside of myself, to be able to look at myself in a situation. I eat really healthy foods most of the time. But I notice on vacation when I had too much caffeine, and when I overate, it influenced the way that I treated other people."

This kind of exploration, with lots of gentleness, self-compassion, and curiosity, can create conditions for insights to arise. What data is coming in through your senses about your relationship with sweet, salty, or healthy foods? Can you be open to deeply listening to the messages your body is sharing with you around food, let them in, and respond skillfully, thereby becoming who you truly are?

Physical Movement

There are as many ways to be active as there are people on this planet. Climate and location can impact what activities you choose; so can physical limitations, such as injuries and disabilities, and gifts, such as balance for skiing, coordination for soccer, or favorable strength-to-weight ratio for rock climbing. And regardless of gifts, most of us can walk, which has scientific evidence to be among the best forms of exercise for physical and mental health. We each have preferences on whether we like to exercise solo, with another person or two, or with a group. Knowing this can help you find a natural fit for physical activity that matches who you are. What is your ideal way?

Using mindfulness to adapt physical activity to fit one's lifestyle is like choosing which plants will thrive best in a particular garden. Skilled gardeners deeply study their land. They investigate how much sand and clay are in the soil, measure the pH of the dirt, watch the sun track across the land to know how much sun and shade the area gets, and learn the rain and temperature patterns in their area. Based on these observations, they plant their garden, selecting species that will naturally thrive in that location. Mindfulness can work in this way, too, with our bodies. A physical activity that fits your lifestyle is one that feels natural for your body and the environment in which you live.

As a teenager hearing about how my grandfather and his brothers excelled at rugby, I wanted to play. I quickly learned that I don't have the physiology or the psyche to be an outstanding rugby player. Being outstanding at a sport is only one reason to do it, and not the best reason, as enjoying an activity and reaping the health and happiness benefits are more important. As I explored different forms of physical activity, I discovered that I had the genetics and psyche to be a fairly high-level triathlete, and more fundamentally, I enjoyed it more. By coming to know myself, I could pick an activity that matched who I was and the environment in which I lived, which included smooth country roads, beautiful running paths, and lakes to swim in. What are the conditions in your body and environment that are suitable to naturally let physical activity happen?

The minimal amount of physical activity for optimal health boils down to thirty to sixty minutes of body work each day: aerobic activity, strength training, stretching, or a combination. And we get a day off once a week or so. It is also good to get up and move at least once an hour. The US Department of Health and Human Services, in collaboration with the National Institutes of Health and the Centers for Disease Control, recommend that adults have least two and a half hours of moderate-intensity aerobic activity or one hour and fifteen minutes of vigorous-intensity aerobic activity every week as well as muscle-strengthening activities at least twice a week (US Department of Health and Human Services 2018).

Just about everyone reports feeling good after physical activity, if it's the right one for them, even hours afterward. Just like with food, this present moment is influenced by prior moments, including exercise. I invite you to notice how you feel before, during, and after physical activity. This is another way to develop your self-awareness (as described in figure 1.1).

Questions for Reflection

How does exercise feel (consider physical sensations, thoughts, emotions):

- a while before exercise (when contemplating it)?
- immediately before exercise (when contemplating it)?
- during exercise?
- one minute after completion?
- twenty minutes after completion?
- one to two hours after completion?
- one day after completion?

What are the types of exercise you like most and least, and why?

We can use mindfulness to turn inward to (1) find what forms of physical activity best suit us, given our genetics and environment; (2) bring mindful awareness to our thoughts, emotions, and physical sensations during the physical activity to maximize enjoyment and performance; and (3) notice how we feel before, during, and after. The latter insight may help motivate us the next time we don't really want to exercise, as often the hardest part is getting started. Once we've started and completed physical activity, it can often feel really good, especially if we connect with points 1 and 2.

Let's try it out in the active contemplation below, either exercising now or at a time in the next few days that works for you. When you do the contemplation, I encourage you to dress in clothes that will allow athletic movement. In the future, if you would prefer to do an activity with others, that's fine, but for now I suggest doing the activity solo so you can concentrate on the body, emotions, and thoughts that are being affected and are affecting the movement.

Physical Activity Meditation

The intention of this meditation is to deepen your understanding of how a specific form of physical activity that you choose impacts your body, emotions, and thoughts—not only while you are doing it, but afterward as well. This present moment is influenced by prior moments, including the physical activity that we have and haven't done.

Taking a moment to connect into your anchor point of the breath, a part of the body, or sound.

Allowing the concentration to settle on this one object.

As thoughts arise, just noticing them, and letting them go, returning back to this moment, and this breath or other object of meditation.

Taking a moment to connect with the body, noticing physical sensations as they arise. Not needing to change them in any way, but just coming to know the body and how it is feeling in this moment.

And now connecting to the emotions and thoughts, noticing what is here in these domains. Even naming silently what emotions are present. Aware of thoughts arising, shifting changing, fading away, and being replaced by new thoughts.

And now, getting ready to engage in a form of physical activity. The encouragement is to do some walking or jogging if your body is capable of that, as it is one of the most natural ways for the body to move. If you prefer another form of moment, such as strength training, brisk house cleaning, yard work, cycling, or swimming, that's okay too.

Notice what is arising in your physical sensations, emotions, and thoughts, knowing that you are about to engage in physical activity. For example, is the heart rate increasing or the palms of the hands beginning to sweat? Is your feeling tone positive, negative, or neutral? What thoughts are here?

Note that we are connecting into the questions in the box above.

The next invitation is to engage in twenty to thirty minutes of physical activity, where the most important goal is to monitor the physical sensations, emotions, and thoughts during the arc of the activity. What is being felt in the body and mind during the activity? Perhaps even seeing if there are ways to modify the activity (such as walking somewhere beautiful, having heart rate in aerobic range where you aren't going too hard but also not too lightly). Allowing the objects of meditation to be the body and the mind during this activity.

As you begin, inviting you to spend a little time warming up the body, so you ease into the activity. Stretching mindfully before or after is welcomed too, if that feels skillful to you.

Inviting you to begin the activity now, with the objects of meditation being your physical sensations, emotions, and thoughts during the entire cycle of the physical activity.

After the activity, taking some time to cool down, if you haven't already. Now either standing or sitting here, taking a moment to connect with the body.

How do the physical sensations feel now compared to before you began the activity?

How about the emotional tone? How is it feeling now compared to when you began?

And the thoughts? What thoughts are here, post-activity?

However you are feeling, just noticing that with curiosity and letting go of self-judgment.

Part of mindfulness is training ourselves to be here with our physical sensations, emotions, and thoughts in a curious, nonjudgmental way, throughout our entire life. Part of life involves physical activity. How does physical activity feel to you, and in bringing your awareness to this, do any insights arise in terms of if and how you would like to bring physical activity into your life differently, or is it good the way you are already bringing it in?

As the meditation comes to a close, taking a moment to return to your anchor point of the breath, body, or sound, as you take a moment to ground yourself before moving onto the next step in your day or evening.

As we bring our awareness to how physical activity makes us feel before, during, and after, we can then respond skillfully to the awareness that arises. This is something we can do with pretty much any behavior, such as our diet or other consumables, including alcohol and other mood-altering substances.

Alcohol and Other Drugs

Alcohol and other mood-altering drugs can foster mind states that allow people to relax, connect with others, or learn about themselves in different ways. And then there are those pesky hangovers and other uncomfortable side effects. Mindfulness allows us to look deeply into our relationship with alcohol and other drugs and see how those agents serve us and others. Is the full arc of the experience—the craving before consuming the intoxicant, the high during consumption, and the hangover afterward—a net benefit for you and those around you? Ask yourself that while using the mindfulness qualities of nonjudgment, curiosity, and gentleness. The answer is simply data. It's not good or bad; it's just information. Does it provide any insights?

Some people use alcohol and other drugs to free themselves from hang-ups—to be able to relax and let go. One of the interesting elements of mindfulness practice is that it illuminates what causes us to constrict (have a hang-up), explore the roots of that constriction with gentleness and curiosity, and then transform those roots to free ourselves. We then become less constricted twenty-four hours a day, rather than just when we are intoxicated. This ability is accessible anytime through concepts such as letting go, liberating the mind, and knowing that everything changes (discussed in more detail in chapter 4).

The beauty of using mindfulness to transform hang-ups is that we can develop the ability to play and let loose without intoxicants. And, we can turn the effects on and off when we want, unlike alcohol or a drug, which needs to run its course and for many of us can lead to addiction. Another element in considering the net benefits and disadvantages in relationship with alcohol and substance use is that it's not just about us as individuals.

The late Joanne Friday, a skilled mindfulness teacher in the Vietnamese Zen Buddhist tradition of Thich Nhat Hanh, once mentioned to me that, as a school counselor, she saw many young people struggling with drug addiction. One student shared with her that he knew of a successful local businessman who smoked pot occasionally, and it didn't seem to affect him in deleterious ways. However, not everyone has success in navigating alcohol and substance use in moderation, including this addicted student who used the businessman as a role model. The point of this story is that we may have our own alcohol or substance use in control, but it is important to recognize that we are also modelling use to others who may have greater predispositions than us to become addicted. We socially influence others in our community.

In fact, research by sociologist Nicholas Christakis, who looked at thousands of participant's data in the Framingham Heart Study, suggested that health behaviors including smoking, weight loss, and even happiness ripple through social networks (Christakis and Fowler 2007, 2008). What are your health behaviors, and how do they influence you and those around you? Again, this is an invitation for you to explore this arena with gentleness, self-kindness, and nonjudgment. Mindfulness practice is used to find the truth in ourselves and our communities. What is the truth in this sphere?

As we bring mindful awareness to behaviors that can have big impacts on our physical well-being and mood, the last one is sleep.

Sleep

A student who attended Oxford University shared that when she set her priorities, she considered the following: "Grades, friends, athletics, and sleep: pick three." In other words, her theory was that you can't have all four. We all know that sleep quality and duration are challenging for many. Research shows sleep quality and quantity are low in many young adults and college students. For example, a study showed that the proportion of college students with sleep difficulties considered "traumatic" or "very difficult to handle" rose from 24 to 31 percent between 2009 and 2017 (Gaultney 2010).

Before the invention of electricity, humans were more likely to shift toward sleep as it got dark. Now, less so. There are many elements of society that promote disturbed sleep, like caffeine, screen time, and sedentary activities. For example, my student Alexa shared, "I was taking melatonin a lot to help me sleep. I recently have been trying to do some of the mindfulness practices before bed. I got off melatonin by doing body scans and listening to the deep relaxation recording, which is very conducive to falling asleep. More physical activity also helps me sleep better, so yoga and mindful walks are probably helping." Alexa learned what contributed to her sleeping better, including physical activity, deep relaxation meditations, and body scans. Some evidence-based factors that promote sleep include going to bed and getting up at the same time each day, avoiding caffeine and alcohol in the evening, and creating a dark and quiet sleeping environment that minimizes distractions (Incze et al. 2018).

In our MBC study, students rated their sleep quality and patterns using the Pittsburgh Sleep Quality Index, which measures sleep quality over a one-month period. Students randomly assigned to take MBC improved their score as the college term progressed. Participants randomly assigned to the control group, which consisted of people who had not taken the course, experienced worsened sleep quality over the school term (Loucks et al. 2021).

Many students have trouble sleeping, and sleep quality is consistently reported to improve by students in mindfulness programs. A contemplation that I offer is called a deep relaxation, which is grounded in a practice offered by Thich Nhat Hanh (2007). If you'd like to try it out, you can find it in chapter 3. You can also find it on the website for this book (http://www.newharbinger.com/49135) if you'd like to listen to it (which is better in a number of ways, as you can fall asleep during the recording, rather than trying to read the meditation and fall asleep).

In this chapter, we explored four big behaviors that influence our health and happiness and for which mindfulness can be effective at optimizing. For many of us, it's just a matter of changing them. And change is not easy, but it is possible and in fact inevitable.

The Burn: Craving and Behavior Change

It's one thing to notice how *we feel* in relation to diet, physical activity, intoxicants, and sleep or to *set an intention* around changing our behaviors. It is quite another *to act* on these feelings and intentions. Resistance to behavior change is fierce. We can get addicted to our brain chemistry, where life might not be great, but we are used to the brain chemistry that our current life creates. This might include, for instance, the highs and lows of caffeine, sugar, and nicotine. There is a familiarity to it that feels normal and comforting, even if it is slowly killing us.

Jud Brewer, an addictions psychiatrist, neuroscientist, and director of research and innovation at Brown's Mindfulness Center, once commented that craving can be a little like a fire in a woodstove. Think of the fire as habit energy, blazing away, doing whatever it is you are used to doing. If you close the damper on the stove, the fire will die down, but it will be trying to suck air through the damper. If you suddenly open the damper (or perhaps give yourself that piece of chocolate or that "quick" check on your social media feed when it's time to be going to sleep), you feed the fire, and it blazes again.

With behavior change, when you stop doing something, even as minor as eating a midafternoon piece of chocolate, there can be an uncomfortable transition time. The craving is there, but just like a fire in a stove, if you keep the damper closed long enough, the fire will die out. If you can keep the new habit going long enough, you will change your brain chemistry to a new set point that is often healthier and happier.

Falling Well

With habit change and goal setting, one of the key elements is knowing how to fall well. We all "fall" or "fail" with our goals, such as by having a binge-drinking session, not exercising for a few days, or eating a pint of ice cream. When that happens, how do you land? Mindfulness encourages gentleness, awareness, nonjudgment, and curiosity.

The times when we aren't practicing mindfulness can be just as informative as the times we are. I invite you to pay attention to how you feel when you fall away from a goal. This is the self-awareness training of mindfulness meditation, which is likely one of the key mechanisms in how it works (figure 1.1). Observe that feeling in a kind, gentle, and curious way. Then, notice what arises in your mind and heart as the skillful next step. Attention-control training, one of the other key mechanisms of mindfulness meditation (figure 1.1), can be helpful with behavior change, as you now have more power to place your mind where you want to. If you realize that you have fallen (such as you ate or drank something that felt detrimental or slept with the wrong person), can you notice that and then use your meditation-induced power of attention control to place your mind on taking the best next step? We can fall skillfully and trust our hearts and minds to illuminate the skillful next actions. The skillful next step might be to choose a different route to work or school that doesn't go by the donut shop, pour the remaining vodka down the sink, or talk with the person you slept with about how you are sorry about the mistake that won't be happening again.

If meditation were easy, everyone would do it. It's not easy. Behavior change isn't either. But it can open up life in major ways. I believe humans are much deeper and tougher than many of us realize and that, by opening to what is in our current experience in a kind way, we can tap into a deep well of energy. I invite you to tap into yours to help you succeed, boost your well-being, and build the life you want.

The main goal of this chapter is to invite you to tap into the body, listen to the messages it shares, and respond skillfully to those messages. A way I have found to do this is to meditate with that as the specific topic. How about we try it now?

Opening the Body Meditation

The intention of this meditation is to check in with your body in a curious and nonjudgmental way and see if it is open—in other words, see if it is feeling good, light, healthy, and free. If the body isn't feeling that way, this meditation offers some prompts to probe into the roots of the body feeling closed, to create opportunities to deeply understand those roots, and to free yourself from those roots. In this way, your body can be more open and healthy, supporting you to live the life you want.

Finding a posture that fosters comfort and wakefulness.

Allowing the eyes to close most of the way, except when peeking to read this contemplation.

Inviting awareness to come right here to this moment, this moment that has never been lived before. Checking in with the mind and the body.

Coming to the anchor point of the breath, the palms of the hands, soles of the feet, or sound.

As thoughts arise, just noticing them, letting them drift along kind of like clouds in a clear blue sky. Coming back to your anchor point so all that's left is this moment, the awareness of this breath, this body, or this sound.

Then inviting awareness to start to shift into a brief body scan. Just checking in, scanning through the body. Starting with the left big toe, inviting awareness to move all the way through the left foot, and continuing through the body at your own pace.

Taking stock of the body and what is here right now, how each and every part of the body is feeling.

Respecting any limits you may have about parts of the body that are overwhelming to be with and skipping those parts, or returning to your anchor point if you feel overwhelmed (or even letting go of this contemplation if it is too much).

This can be a relatively rapid body scan.

What we are doing here is fostering our attention-control to place our mind where we want to place it and fostering our self-awareness, particularly of the body.

And then holding that whole body in awareness everywhere from the tips of the toes to the top of the head and everywhere in between.

Inviting the question, Is the body open?

For example: Do your muscles feel exercised and strong? Do your joints and ligaments feel limber? Are the effects of the food you had letting your body burn cleanly? Do you have a lack of hangover? A full tank from your sleep? Is the body open? Is it free? Is it vibrant? Does it have energy to it?

And if not, why not?

Is the body feeling closed in any way? If it is, that's just good information. Taking a moment to be here with it and caring for it in a nonjudgmental way, kind of like a parent would care for a crying child. After time, once it settles, can you see the roots of what is causing it to be constricted or agitated?

Are any closures or agitation related to what you ate or didn't eat? To the physical activity you've had or not had? To the substance you've been consuming or to the sleep you have or haven't been getting? Is it something else?

And if the body is feeling open, what are the roots of why it is feeling open?

That's really good information.

Once you know what is causing the body to constrict or not be open, or alternatively to be open and vibrant, that is a major step. Allowing those root causes to settle in.

And then seeing if any insights arise in terms of the next skillful steps.

Inviting you to picture what life would be like if you took those next steps.

If it looks like a net benefit, then inviting you with your training in attention control to place your mind and body in the direction of taking those skillful next steps.

In the home practice below, the first practice will give you some more structure to take steps on the intentions that may have arisen for you.

One morning during meditation, when I asked myself if my body was open, I could feel that my body needed exercise—particularly my upper body, as I used my lower body and core muscles during a hike the day before. I responded by doing some push-ups, chin-ups (on a tree branch), and burpees while I was away from my home gym, visiting my parents. After those ten to fifteen minutes of strength training, my body felt more open and healthy, and my emotions and mind felt better too.

Tuning in to taking care of what opens your body can lead to a healthier body, and in turn a healthier heart and mind. In the next chapter, we focus on opening the heart; in particular, we're going to tap into our emotional well-being.

Home Practices

The practices offered in the book, if done regularly, have the capacity to change your body and mind in healthy ways. Below are some practices that you are invited to engage with this week.

1. I invite you to look deeply within to learn what you hope for in the domain of your physical health.

    First, sitting with the eyes mostly closed and then perhaps starting to check in with the breath (or another anchor point), bringing awareness to the sensation of it coming in and out as the diaphragm pulls down and releases up.

    Allowing the thoughts to settle and noticing where the mind goes. Each time attention drifts away from the breath, inviting it back with kindness and firmness.

    Doing this for a couple minutes and then shifting to noticing what is in your physical sensations.

    What is your body sharing with you right now? Can you listen to what that message is?

If your body isn't sharing much, then just recognizing that it isn't sharing much.

In the domain of your physical health, is there anything there that you want for yourself? It's your true self, deep within, that is invited to come out. Maybe it is a strong desire to let go of eating sugar, a desire to be fit enough to run a 10K race, or a wanting to be more attractive for yourself and a potential romantic partner by taking care of your body through diet, exercise, and sleep. Maybe it is knowing that you often feel hungover after a night of alcohol or substance use and knowing that reducing those substances would benefit you. Maybe it's sleep, and by not getting enough, you find yourself in a cycle the next day of sugar and coffee to make up for it, which only has you sleeping worse that night and renewing the cycle the next day.

Whatever it is, what is your true self that wants to come out? Can you let it out?

I invite you to answer the questions below. This is an evidence-informed approach similar to motivational interviewing to promote positive behavior change.

What is your intention related to diet, alcohol consumption, physical activity, sleep, or some other physical-health-related realm for the coming week?

A. On a scale of 1 to 10, where 10 is high, how *motivated* are you to achieve this intention?

B. On a scale of 1 to 10, how *confident* are you that you will achieve the intention?

C. What could you do that would raise your motivation or confidence a little?

D. What might make it difficult to achieve the intention this week, and if that happens, what will you do?

E. How could you measure this intention in a way that resonates with you?

I welcome you to share this intention with someone, such as a parent or friend, as having that social support sometimes helps to act on the goal.

2. You learned that there are two major forms of meditation practice: focused attention and open monitoring. While both forms are beneficial, focused attention, especially at first, may be particularly effective at fostering well-being quickly. I invite you to do an attentional-focus practice just about every day this week. On the book's website (http://www.newharbinger.com/49135), you will find recordings of different lengths if you'd like a guided one, or you can also just refer to the first guided meditation in this chapter.

3. Every other day, I invite you to practice one of the other meditations in this chapter, such as the body scan, mindful eating, mindful physical activity, or opening the body. I encourage you to pick one that most resonates with you.

CHAPTER 2

Opening the Heart

Becoming More Aware of, and Skillfully Using, Your Emotions

"There was a boy I dated a few years ago," explained Sabrina, a young adult who went through one of my mindfulness courses. "Recently, we hung out and kissed for the first time in a long time. As I walked home from his house, I noticed I was almost skipping. I noticed I was happy. I realized that I am now so much more aware of my thoughts and feelings. When I feel anxious or sad, I experience it to a fuller extent. The highs are definitely higher, but the lows are lower as well." As Sabrina discovered, mindfulness can help us feel our emotions more clearly and respond to them.

I remember MBSR teacher-trainer Lynn Koerbel once asking students, Wouldn't it be nice if we could just open one side of the heart? To just the positive things? However, she shared, when we open the heart, it all tends to open, so we can be here with all emotions, hold them, and work with them as is called for.

Sabrina intuitively understood this when she said, "I am an introvert, so when I spent time with friends, I would often have low energy and need more time to myself. Now that I am more mindful, I notice that my energy dips more than I realized. Because of the mindfulness and meditation training, I recognize when I need time alone. In the past, when I noticed my energy dipping, I would fight it. If my friends were going to dinner, I'd force myself to go. It turns out when I would do that, the night would not turn out well for me. I now know I need an hour or a few hours or the whole night to recuperate. Now I go for a twenty-minute run, or journal and meditate. It is an anchor for me."

Sabrina went on to describe a specific example. "A couple of weeks ago there was a group of friends that wanted to go out to dinner, drink, and go to a friend's house. It was going to be, relatively speaking, a 'big night.' I remember waking up and feeling low energy. I tried in the afternoon to take care of myself—nap, run, meditate. I started to get dressed to go out. I knew I wasn't up for it, so I stayed in and made myself dinner. Once I finished eating, I started to feel better. I was feeling up to joining my friends. If I had met them for dinner, I would have been miserable, and that would have continued. By taking that hour to myself, I was in a much better space and could actually enjoy the evening. I was able to be present with them and not in my head." Sabrina's mindfulness practice has taught her to know herself better, and in doing so, she's become a more engaged and grounded friend.

There's a lot of focus on emotional health these days due to factors like large student loans, high housing costs, job instability, the pushes and pulls of social media and other digital platforms; cheap, easily accessible, tasty, processed foods that influence mood; sedentary activities; social isolation; sleep challenges that influence mental well-being; along with fears about environmental collapse and climate change; not to mention, at the time of writing this book, a pandemic. We are often not taught much in school or our families about how to competently work with emotions, so we don't have the skills or know where to get them. Mindfulness can help with emotional regulation.

In this chapter, I offer several tools you can use to tap into your emotional wisdom, listen to the messages there, harness your emotions, and skillfully respond to the emotional messages present. The tools and concepts in this chapter can contribute to overall emotional well-being, including happiness and joy—what many are referring to as "flourishing." Part of flourishing in many ways is having an open heart.

What Is an Open Heart?

I was once in a room with some of the leading scientists and scholars on mindfulness working to agree on a consensus definition of mindfulness. It was destabilizing, and in some ways empowering, to hear the lack of consistent definitions offered. In *Mindfulness: Ancient Wisdom Meets Modern Psychology,* Oxford professor Willem Kuyken and dharma teacher Christina Feldman (2019) offer no less than nine definitions of and thirteen metaphors for mindfulness.

Defining mindfulness may be similar to defining an open heart. I can provide some indication with words, as I did in the introduction, but it is really a personal experience that will be unique to you. In fact, the Buddha is credited as saying, "The teaching is merely a vehicle to describe the truth. Don't mistake it for the truth itself. A finger pointing at the moon is not the moon. The finger is needed to know where to look for the moon, but if you mistake the finger for the moon itself, you will never know the real moon" (Nhat Hanh 1987).

Don't mistake the finger for the moon. In this book, words like "mindfulness" and "open heart" are fingers pointing at the moon. All around the world, if people feel something meaningful, they often place their hand on their heart. Even the term "heart-warming" is similar to opening the heart. The term "open mind," which we will touch on in the next chapter, refers to being open to new ideas and what is "here." An open heart is similar in that we are emotionally aware and open to what is here.

What conditions open the heart? And can we foster them to happen? One element that allows for heart openings is caring for the body's basic needs for optimal functioning (healthy diet, physical activity, sleep), as described in the prior chapter. If we have had enough sleep and take care of our body through diet and exercise, we are more likely to be emotionally ripe for openings to occur. For example, evidence shows that healthy diets, including adequate vegetable intake, are associated with more positive emotions and lower depression symptoms over time (Molendijk et al.

2018). Physical activity, particularly when commuting to work or during leisure-time, also enhances mood (White et al. 2017). A recent study showed that exercise might even help provide resilience to stressors, such as social conflict and job stress (Thomas et al. 2019). An element that causes heart openings is connecting with others. By getting to know your mind and body and what opens your heart, you can introduce those conditions more often and watch your heart spend more time open.

Connecting the Open Heart and Body

Qualitative analyses in mindfulness studies showed how caring for our emotions influences caring for our bodies, and vice-versa (for example Nardi et al. 2020). For example, an MBC participant shared, "I can feel when I'm elevated and super tense, and I can also physically choose how to lower that, whether it's doing some physical exercise, breathing, meditating, or yoga, or through what I eat."

Throughout this book, you'll see evidence that an open body and an open heart support each other and synergize by being stronger together than apart. We'll also explore the concepts of an open mind and an open spirit in the coming chapters. All of these contribute, and interact with each other, to foster your success, boost your well-being, and build the life you want.

Opening the Heart through the Discourse on Breathing Mindfulness

Now, let's return to the Discourse on Breathing Mindfulness. The second four contemplations are focused on the emotions or "feeling tones." Feeling tones, or *vedanā* in Pāli, are the valence of emotions, specifically positive (pleasant, nice, agreeable), negative (unpleasant, disagreeable, painful), and neutral (neither pleasant nor unpleasant) emotional tones (Buddhadāsa Bhikkhu 1988). In these four contemplations, we are working to foster positive emotions, such as contentment, satisfaction, and rapture, that arise when we are successful at something.

In this set of contemplations, we begin to become more aware of our emotions, moment by moment, and then in turn calm them and care for them. In doing so, we may find ourselves more self-aware and self-expressed. We may also find that we become more emotionally healthy as we learn skills to be more sensitive to detecting what our emotional tone is moment to moment and have greater capacity to care for and respond to the emotions in wise ways. Opening our heart and caring for our emotions can provide with greater emotional depth and resilience to in turn better care for others.

DISCOURSE ON BREATHING MINDFULNESS:
Second Tetrad of Contemplations

5. *Breathing in, I feel joyful. Breathing out, I feel joyful.*

6. *Breathing in, I feel happy. Breathing out, I feel happy.*

7. *Breathing in, I am aware of my mental formations (emotions). Breathing out, I am aware of my mental formations.*

8. *Breathing in, I calm my mental formations (emotions). Breathing out, I calm my mental formations.*

The contemplations in Discourse on Breathing Mindfulness are typically done in order, as I present them in this book. As you work with the contemplations, I encourage you to always start with the first one (*Breathing in, I know I am breathing in...*) and then progress through in order to the one you are currently focusing on. (You can find all sixteen in appendix 2.) As you're learning them though, we'll discuss them individually, so let's look at the fifth contemplation.

Fostering Joy

DISCOURSE ON BREATHING MINDFULNESS:
Fifth Contemplation

5. *Breathing in, I feel joyful. Breathing out, I feel joyful.*

I don't know about you, but when I first read "I feel joyful," I railed against it. I thought to myself, *I am not going to artificially feel joy unless it naturally arises. I'm not going to force an emotion. That just feels fake. And a little touchy-feely. I'm good if it arises naturally though.*

In Bhikkhu Anālayo's (2019) commentary on the Discourse of Breathing Mindfulness, he shares, "With the momentum of the previous practices and based on the deep relaxation brought about by the preceding step of calming bodily activity, at the present juncture, joy can often arise quite spontaneously, at least in a subtle form. All that is required is to recognize even rather delicate manifestations of joy." In other words, the first tetrad of the Discourse described in chapter 1, which brings awareness to in-breath and out-breath and calms and cares for the body, can at times naturally lead to feelings of joy.

Another way that we can foster joy has been taught by Thich Nhat Hanh (1991), who wrote about the joy of a non-toothache. If you've ever had an injury, whether it was a toothache, a hangnail, or a broken bone, you can probably relate to the joy you would feel if it were no longer injured. That joy is accessible any time. For example, if you don't have a toothache now, can you feel some joy in that? Do you have use of your eyes? Consider the joy in realizing that, especially if you know someone who doesn't. The same is true for taste and smell. Are you breathing clean air? Are you able to breathe without oxygen assistance as someone with COVID or COPD may need? The point of this contemplation is that there are almost always opportunities to deliberately foster joy. These positive emotions that have an element of excitedness to them are known as *pīti* in Pāli.

If you are like me, your mind often, when left to its own devices, lands somewhere that is related to a problem. In many ways, anthropologically, our ancestors survived because they were able to detect problems and avoid or fix them. Humans as a species are set up to do that, and part of flourishing and opening the heart is to work deliberately on the areas that need a tune-up. For many of us, fostering joy is one of those areas. Bhikkhu Anālayo (2019) offered a tool to create an aspiration for joy, such as saying or thinking, "May joy arise," encouraging joy to be offered to ourselves in a reverential manner.

As we consider the value of fostering joy, from a trauma-informed perspective, or to minimize adverse effects of meditation, deliberately fostering joy and happiness before contemplations seven and eight above can help set us up for a more resilient, comfortable experience being with our emotions. For example, a depressed feeling can involve a repetitive cycle of negative thoughts that can be difficult to get out of. Evidence has shown that mindfulness-based programs improve mental health in part by helping people stop repetitive negative thinking (Gu et al. 2015) and instead direct their attention to a place that better serves them in each moment. In some ways, that is what we are doing here too. It's okay to have negative emotions and thoughts, just as it is okay to have neutral and positive ones. But the suggestion in this moment is to see if we notice what fosters joy in ourselves, even if it something as simple as the smile of a child, a flower in a garden, or a blue sky. That joy can often lead in time to happiness.

Fostering Happiness

DISCOURSE ON BREATHING MINDFULNESS:
Sixth Contemplation

6. *Breathing in, I feel happy. Breathing out, I feel happy.*

Imagine someone in a desert who has been walking for days and then sees on the horizon an oasis that they know has fresh water. An initial feeling they might experience is joy (or *pīti*, which in this case could be rapture with an excited element to it). When they drink the water, that feeling might be *happiness*, or in Pāli, *sukha*. *Sukha* is translated as happiness, bliss, tranquil, and soothing. It has a pleasant, calming aspect to it. In this contemplation, we are fostering *sukha*, or happiness, in ourselves.

Knowing what brings you happiness is important because in knowing it, we can either deliberately bring more of those elements into our lives or just get better at recognizing and being grateful for the factors already in our lives that provide *sukha*. We can do this when we would appreciate our emotional tone to be more pleasant. What is it that brings happiness to you? Is it a connection to a family member, friend, romantic partner, or classmate? Is it giving a gift of your time to a particular cause or group? Perhaps getting some exercise or having your favorite cup of tea?

This set of contemplations focuses on "mind-conditioners," or how our emotions influence, or "condition" our mind, such as our thoughts (Buddhadāsa Bhikkhu 1988). If there is an emotional tone of happiness present, for example, that happy feeling usually influences our thoughts (and actions) in a unique way compared to if we had a different emotional tone, say, of anger. We will turn to the mind-conditioners, or awareness of emotions, more in the seventh contemplation.

Emotional Self-Awareness

DISCOURSE ON BREATHING MINDFULNESS:
Seventh Contemplation

7. *Breathing in, I am aware of my mental formations (emotions). Breathing out, I am aware of my mental formations.*

Another translation of this contemplation is *"Breathing in, I am aware of my mind-conditioners. Breathing out, I am aware of my mind-conditioners"* (Buddhadāsa Bhikkhu 1988).

Just like there are many more words for *snow* in Inuit languages compared to English because the Inuit people have come to know snow so thoroughly and snow conditions are important to their livelihood and well-being, so too there are many nuanced, rich words in Pāli related to conditions of the mind that don't translate completely into English. You've probably noticed that I have referred to emotions using a few different words ("mind-conditioners") to provide a richer context to what is really being referred to here. "Mental formations" is another one. Depending on the Buddhist tradition, there about fifty-two different mental formations, also known as "mind formations." One of them is emotions (*vedanā)*. Others are attention, perception, delusion, greed, envy, mindfulness, tranquility, compassion, and wisdom.

Awareness of our emotions, or mind-conditioners, can help us see clearly how deleterious factors, such as addiction, influence our lives and give us the energy to change them. For example, Paul shared, "When I put a substance of any kind in my body that feels good, it tends to set of chain of events into action that doesn't make me feel good. Even the first one turns me into someone I don't want to be. There's this saying, 'There're certain things that control is impossible the moment it's suggested.' That's alcohol and drugs for me. When addiction was manifesting itself in heavy ways for me, I think I was looking for something. I was looking for something the world isn't offering—something that made me feel whole and connected. The practice of mindfulness is the most direct route to that feeling. It takes some hard work, courage, and commitment, but there is no moment at which it's not possible."

Through Paul's self-awareness of his emotional tone, he was able to see how much better meditation made him feel overall compared to alcohol and drugs. Through this realization, he came to care for his emotions by fostering a personal mindfulness and meditation practice and acting on the insights that arose from it. There are specific practices that encourage us to take a moment to pause, check in with our emotional tone, and respond to that emotional tone in a considered way. One approach that we teach in MBSR and MBC is the STOP practice.

The STOP Mindfulness Practice

One way to connect with our emotions and emotional wisdom is to use the STOP practice. The STOP practice can be used periodically throughout the day. It's a useful habit to get into. Evidence suggests that it helps with emotion regulation, especially when feeling depressed, anxious, or stressed. But you can use it any time, as it is good training for being "here" every moment, whether that moment is pleasant, unpleasant, or somewhere in between.

Here's how to do the STOP practice:

S: Stop what you are doing.

T: Take a breath.

O: Observe and open to thoughts, feelings, and the physical manifestations of the experience (tension in shoulders, for example).

P: Proceed by doing something to support an effective response to the experience. This might include skillfully responding to someone who just asked you to do something, taking a short walk to take some space from what just occurred, hugging that family member or friend who just smiled at you, or deciding not to have another alcoholic beverage.

In our research, the STOP practice was frequently reported as useful. One participant shared: "Alarm bells go off in my head, and I know I need to stop, take a breath, open toward me, and proceed. And then I remember to be kind to myself."

   The STOP practice can help regulate strong emotions. The MBC study showed significant protective effects against depression over the school term. In the people randomly assigned to be in the control group (who waited to take the course until the following term), depressive symptoms increased as exams and term papers mounted (figure 2.1). The people randomly assigned to take the Mindfulness-Based College course, while facing the same stressors, showed resilience. Their depressive symptoms stayed stable in the face of the term's stressors (Loucks et al. 2021). Other mindfulness studies in youths (ages twelve to twenty-five years) showed similar findings (Dawson et al. 2019).

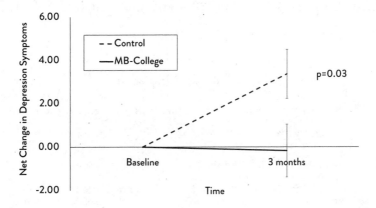

Figure 2.1 Changes in depression symptoms (according to the Center for Epidemiologic Studies Depression's scale score) from the beginning to the end of the college term, as stressors rise with impending final exams and term papers. Participants were randomized to (1) Mindfulness-Based College or (2) a control group that received mental health services if needed and waited to take the course until the following term. There were significant (p=0.03) between-group differences at the three-month follow up.

   I invite you to take a few opportunities each day to STOP—not only when you are feeling stressed or unsure but as a way to be in the moment, whether to feel the beautiful sun shining on your face, fully notice the smile of a child, or feel the sadness in your heart. A big part of mindfulness is coming to know yourself, including where your emotions are at right now, recognizing that emotions may shift from moment to moment or have steadiness. One of the best ways to come to know our emotions better, and thereby care and harness them to serve ourselves and others, is to stop and observe our feelings with curiosity, gentleness, and kindness. I invite you to try the STOP practice now before going on to the next section. That section will focus on calming and caring for our emotions, but it is a challenge to calm or care for our emotions if we don't really know what they are. The seventh contemplation above, and the STOP practice, help us do so.

Calming and Caring for Our Emotions

DISCOURSE ON BREATHING MINDFULNESS:
Eighth Contemplation

8. *Breathing in, I calm my mental formations (emotions). Breathing out, I calm my mental formations.*

I tend to adapt it as: "Breathing in, I calm my emotions. Breathing out, I care for my emotions."

In the context of this contemplation, a calming of the emotions can be a natural result of engaging in the first seven contemplations. After we have cared for the body (in the first four contemplations), then fostered *pīti* and *sukha* (in the fifth and sixth contemplations), and connected with the emotional tone (in the seventh contemplation), we may see that our emotions have naturally become calmer. In my experience, it is also an opportunity to care for the emotions that are present, wherever they are on the spectrum of negative to positive.

Mindfulness practice often leads to better self-care habits and a greater desire to care for ourselves. As we begin to practice mindfulness, using mindfulness qualities of gentleness, curiosity, and nonjudgment, we come to know ourselves better because we are spending more time with our thoughts, emotions, and sensations. In doing so, we often want to care for ourselves more. In fact, self-kindness is an element that many participants report developing after beginning a mindfulness practice.

Many people are hard on themselves without realizing how much it affects their mood. They beat themselves up with a sometimes-ruthless inner dialogue. By mindfully considering two simple tactics—self-kindness and self-care—we can move away from being self-critical, angry, or sad to accepting. Jayden, a former student, is a case in point.

Jayden, as a young adult, lived most of his life feeling as if he wasn't good enough. There was always something he could improve. He started using drugs to escape these uncomfortable feelings. Although Jayden had been in a meaningful relationship, he didn't tell his partner about his drug use. His partner's oblivion ended when Jayden was hospitalized for a suicide attempt.

Afterward, Jayden and his partner, David, saw a therapist. The therapist asked Jayden what he was happy about with himself. There was absolutely nothing Jayden could name. So, his therapist tried a different approach. She asked, "What do you think David loves about you? Why is he with you? Why would he choose to stick next to a guy like you?" Jayden couldn't answer those questions. He remembered sitting on the therapist's couch crying and not having a clue about what he had that was of value.

Jayden's therapist was one of the first people to talk with him about self-kindness. She told him to wake up in the morning and think of something he was happy about rather than all things he wasn't. He began to engage in mindfulness training. One of the clearest self-kindness stories Jayden described had to do with taking his daily medication that was important to his well-being. Before learning about self-kindness, Jayden would take the medication every morning and feel down about his life because he'd think of the reasons he needed to take it. "The medications were a constant reminder that I have this disease. Jayden started to care for his emotions and see this medicine as a gift from the researchers who developed it.

Jayden is grateful to the people who developed and tested the medications that now allow for much greater well-being than was previously possible. Taking the medication has become an act of gratitude and kindness to himself. Because he's no longer resisting or dreading this part of his daily routine, he remembers to take his medication, further affirming his feelings of self-worth. Emotionally, he feels more balanced and grounded and even happier. Jayden is an example of self-kindness. We can also offer kindness, or what is known as "loving-kindness," to others.

Loving-Kindness

Loving-kindness is just what it sounds like. It is offering tender and benevolent affection toward ourselves or others (Salzberg 2002). "Metta" is a Pāli term that means benevolence, loving-kindness, friendliness, good will, and active interest in others. It is often translated as "loving-kindness." Practicing loving-kindness opens us up, giving us a greater capacity to forgive and realize how connected we are—not only to other people but to nature and, really, to everything.

Lan Anh, one of my students, found that practicing loving-kindness meditation allowed a change in her relationship with her father. During loving-kindness meditation, whenever she needed to come up with a person that she had difficulty with, she would think of her father. It was hard for her because she had a lot of resentment and anger toward him. While growing up in Vietnam, Lan Anh only saw him once or twice a month. She experienced her dad as financially irresponsible and emotionally abusive to her family. When she heard that her paternal grandmother passed away, she felt sad for her father, particularly when she thought about how important her own mom was to her.

One night, she found herself forgiving her father for all he had done. She shared that without loving-kindness meditation, she would not have been able to let go of that resentment and forgive him. It was as if she let go of a knot inside herself. Lan Anh is now able to talk to her dad again as a daughter without feeling held back, whether it is by the anger or self-judgment. As she shared, "And now I can genuinely care for my dad. My care for him is much more authentic now. I think of him as my father and someone I can care for—rather than before, where it was forced, thinking, *This is my dad, and I have to care for him in my role as his daughter.*" Lan Anh summed it up well when she said, "I have moved out of my glass prison, and he is no longer the difficult person that I work with."

Loving-Kindness Meditation

The intention of this meditation is to foster your ability to stay grounded and centered when offering loving-kindness to yourself and others. It is designed for you to work out the regions of the nervous system that operate your ability to be kind and friendly to yourself and other beings. So much of humans' abilities to flourish, including excelling in the workplace and family life, is based on our ability to collaborate, understand the needs of those that we serve, and meet those needs—all while taking care of ourselves so we are happy and healthy in the process and can live our lives to the fullest. This meditation should help you bat that out of the park.

I will lead you through the basics of a loving-kindness meditation now so you have it in your menu of mindfulness practices. As you progress through it, just remember to take care of yourself. The meditation asks you to offer loving-kindness to yourself, to those you have a caring easy relationship with, to people who are neutral, and to those whom you have a difficult time with. As you pick your difficult person, consider picking one who offers you an opportunity for personal growth (building character, as I often tell my daughters) but is not overwhelming. As you offer them loving-kindness, just remember that you aren't necessarily forgiving them, but just offering them well-wishing.

I find one of the people that is most common to have difficulties offering loving-kindness to is ourselves. When tears have come in class members when I lead this, they are often due to catharsis, or regrets of the past, in offering kindness to ourselves. I have had a number of women in their sixties and seventies during our all-day retreats, share that never in their lives have they spent a whole day caring for themselves; they have always been focused on caring for others. For you as a young adult, you have the opportunity to get this sorted out earlier in life. In doing so, by taking this time to offer loving-kindness and care to yourself, you will likely find that your capacity to care for others is strengthened, as you will be healthier and happier and thereby have more energy and groundedness when you are serving others. Let's try it out, if you like.

> Inviting you to start with a grounded, focused meditation on an anchor point, such as the in-breath and out-breath, perhaps noticing where the breath first comes in and last leaves the body, at the nose or the mouth. Being aware of the sensations, and letting other thoughts drop away. Coming back to this moment and this breath. This breath that's never been breathed before.
>
> After you have settled and brought your concentration more into the present moment (say five minutes or so), you are invited to bring awareness and kindness toward yourself. The invitation is to offer these upcoming contemplations kind of like a gift. Inviting you to let go of judgment ("May I be happy," is encouraged rather than, "I should be happier. Why aren't I happier?") and just offer this gift from a place of kindness. You can even try the following contemplations, or feel free to adapt them to best resonate with you:
>
> May I be safe and healthy.
>
> May I have ease of body and mind.
>
> May I be at peace.
>
> Noticing your physical sensations, emotions, and thoughts as you offer these words of loving-kindness to yourself. How does it feel? For many of us, offering kindness to ourselves is unusual, and if that is the case, that's good information. Just noticing your experience with kindness, gentleness, and care.

Bringing someone to mind whom you have an easy relationship with and whom you care for a lot. Maybe it is a teacher, a parent, a loved one, or even a pet. Now offering loving-kindness toward that being:

May they be safe and healthy.

May they have ease of body and mind.

May this person (or animal) be at peace.

What is your emotional tone? How does it feel to be offering these phrases to this person (or animal)? For many of us, it feels quite easy and full, as we care so much about them.

Shifting now to someone neutral, maybe your postal carrier or someone who bags your groceries. Maybe someone you see in class or at work, but don't really feel affection or aversion toward. Holding that person in mind and offering loving-kindness toward them:

May they be safe and healthy.

May this person have ease of body and mind.

May they be at peace.

Noticing how it feels to offer these phrases to the person, compared to when you offered them to yourself or someone you have an easy relationship with. How is it different, if it is different? How is it similar, if it is similar? That's good information to know as you come to understand yourself in this way, in relation to other people.

Next, the invitation is to bring to mind someone you have aversion toward, perhaps a family member or someone at school or work you find challenging. Remember that you aren't necessarily forgiving this person, just offering kindness. Here, you may want to respect your limits and work with someone juicy enough to provide a rich experience but not an overwhelming one. First, offering kindness to yourself for your choice, then bringing to mind that person and offering loving-kindness toward them. Being aware, with kindness and gentleness, of how it feels for you to offer loving-kindness in this way to this person, compared with offering it to others, such as the loved or neutral person.

The final opportunity is to expand out. Holding in mind everyone in the room (or whatever surrounds you, such as the building or park) and everyone in the neighborhood, and continuing to expand out by holding in your heart and mind everyone in the city, the state, the country, the continent, and the world. If you like, perhaps including all the animals, plants, and even minerals. Then offering loving-kindness as you feel comfortable:

May all beings be safe and healthy.

May everyone have ease of body and mind.

May we all be at peace.

Noticing how it feels to offer this loving-kindness more broadly.

Loving-kindness practice can be powerful. How mindfulness practice influences your life when you are not meditating is where it counts the most. Explore if, and how, loving-kindness influences you on the days that you practice it. Some people report being more balanced when communicating. For example, some people may "lose" themselves in the process of doing something for others. You may find that practicing loving-kindness regularly allows communications to be more authentic, direct, and honest, not only with others but with yourself.

Starting the day in a quiet space where you can sit comfortably and bring to mind people whom you feel close to, neutral to, and have an aversion to can allow you to stay connected with your mind and body later in the day when you are actually communicating with the people in your life. You may find that it allows you to move away from overwhelming thoughts more easily than when you are physically with these people versus with them only in thought.

This loving-kindness training is akin to going to the gym to work out your relationality muscles, and like a good workout, it can translate into the rest of the day. But, that's just my perspective. What does loving-kindness practice do for you?

Staying Emotionally Safe

In MBSR and MBC, we refer to three zones of stress and well-being: the comfort zone, growth zone (eustress), and overwhelmed zone (distress) (figure 2.2). Eustress is the good kind of stress that allows us to learn and grow and be motivated, such as the pressure you might feel when writing a term paper that's due in a few weeks and that could bolster your grade point. Distress is when stress gets overwhelming and beyond your ability to cope—perhaps starting a term paper that's due the next day.

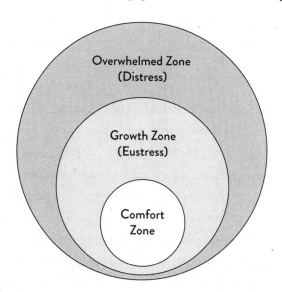

Figure 2.2 Zones of comfort, growth, and overwhelm, and how the former two expand with mindfulness training.

Distress can be short term, as in the example of the term paper, or more chronic, as is the case with ongoing depression or anxiety. If you are distressed, or find yourself in the overwhelmed zone for too long, a coping strategy can help ground you back into either the comfort or eustress zone for a period of time so you can once again fill your tank of resilience. There are three key coping strategies:

- mindfulness

- distraction (for example, going to the gym to work out if over-whelmed by a stressful interaction with a family member)

- behavior (for example, taking a pain-relieving medication for overwhelming pain)

All three coping strategies can be used skillfully. While behavior and distraction often get the fastest results, mindfulness is longer lasting and informs other areas of life, offering great insights when we turn toward the difficulty. The best strategy for you may vary in any given moment and in different situations.

For example, one night, I woke up at about three o'clock in the morning and checked my newsfeed. There, I received some upsetting information. I was so stressed that it activated my sympathetic nervous system, providing a surge of adrenalin. I was not going back to sleep. I got up, headed downstairs, sat on my cushion, and meditated, sometimes looking through the windows at the cedar and pine trees above. I sat there for a couple hours, with mindful awareness, being with my thoughts, emotions, and sensations in a nonjudgmental, curious way.

I was tired, and my meditation attempt wasn't working well. I'd been awake long enough that the gym was open, so I drove over and funneled the frustration and anger into one of the better workouts I'd had in a while. By distracting myself in a way that was also healthy for me, I was able to take a step back and fill my tank of well-being. Consequently, I came home more grounded and balanced to meet my waking wife and daughters and hold them while I shared the upsetting news.

With mindfulness, you're invited at times to come closer to the feelings of stress, often as eustress (the growth zone) but also dipping into the distress for brief periods. It can be skillful to come closer to the difficulty to see what's there. Moving toward the suffering and observing it with kindness and gentleness often allows for insights to arise that can help you to shift your well-being.

Sometimes, however, moving toward the suffering can flip us into an overwhelmed state, which is when healthy distraction or behaviors can help ground us back into the comfort zone or growth/eustress zone so we can once again fill our tank of well-being and resilience.

Adverse events with mindfulness practice are sometimes reported. While the evidence is minimal for mindfulness-based programs, such as MBSR and MBCT, so far findings suggest that there are similar adverse events in both the mindfulness-based program and control conditions, suggesting mindfulness-based programs are unlikely to induce adverse events any more than if participants didn't take the program (Baer et al. 2019). Still, the evidence is minimal and not conclusive. More resources are becoming available, such as the book *Trauma-Sensitive Mindfulness* by David Treleavan. Experts, including Willoughby Britton and Jared Lindahl at Brown University, are looking into adverse events in meditation practices (Lindahl et al. 2017) and provide resources to meditators in distress through their nonprofit organization Cheetah House (http://cheetahhouse.org).

In our MBC randomized controlled trial (Loucks et al. 2021),[8] three participants in the control group and one person in the MBC group reported adverse events. The MBC-group adverse event was depression and anxiety, attributed to a major injury in this college athlete. One of the adverse events in the control group was suicidal ideation. However, when the student took the MBC course after the trial, he shared that it made positive differences in his life.

Difficult experiences can arise with meditation, and if they do for you, just know that you are not alone and that there are professionals, such as counselors, psychologists, family doctors, and skilled mindfulness instructors, who can support you. In the meantime, I recommend simply noticing how the mindfulness practices feel to you. If they are helpful, then keep using them. If they aren't, then let them go. There are many paths to health and happiness.

Opening the Heart

Two of the goals of this chapter were to help you develop self-awareness to notice your emotional tone and to develop emotion regulation skills to care for your emotions. We often feel emotions in the heart area, especially if we are feeling open. So, an easy way to check in about your emotional tone is to ask yourself, "Is my heart open?" The key is to offer yourself lots of self-care and nonjudgment in the process. And if your answer is no, ask, "Why not?" The question "Why not?" allows you to understand the roots of why your emotions are as they are. Once we understand the roots, the path forward to heal can become clearer.

For one of my students, the path forward was working with a therapist to talk through the emotions of past traumatic experiences that had become more at the forefront through the meditation practices. She knew that she could heal through a combination of psychological therapy and mindfulness training. For Jayden, it was practicing self-kindness. For me, loving-kindness is often very effective for opening my heart, as is making sure that my body is taken care of (specifically avoiding coffee and sugar and starting my day with physical activity). What is it that might help you to shift to spending more time with an open heart? Below is a meditation on opening the heart.

Opening the Heart Meditation

The intention of this meditation is to connect with the emotions to see if they are clenched or closed down in any way. If so, the meditation guides us to explore what the roots of the closure are. By understanding the roots, often a skillful path forward arises that can give us a healthier, happier emotional tone, letting us be who we truly are. This can support us to engage with the world in a more open way that better harnesses our entire self by being aware of, caring for, and harnessing our emotions. Emotions are there for a good reason and provide us with important information on how and who we are and what we can best do to care for ourselves and others.

I like to start this practice with an anchoring practice. Once we are anchored, having fostered our concentration and attention control, we can broaden out to connect with the body (chapter 1) and then move up to the emotions and the heart.

Finding a position to settle in for a meditation that is comfortable and promotes alertness. Closing the eyes most of the way and finding your way to your anchor point. Noticing the in-breath and out-breath. Seeing how deep or shallow the breath is or how fast or slow it is. Not needing to change it in any way but just coming to know it better. If your anchor is sound, noticing raw elements, like pitch, volume, and frequency.

Taking time to be here with this moment, this moment that has never happened before.

Being here with the mind and the body.

Inviting concentration to rest on the object of meditation—the breath, body, or sound.

Knowing that you always have your anchor point to come back to, the invitation is to start to connect in with the sensations of the body. Letting in awareness of the body and seeing what messages are there in the body. If the messages are overwhelming, you can come back to the anchor of the breath, a particular region of the body, or sound.

Noticing the body and how it is today. Offering it curiosity and acceptance. The invitation, if you like, is offering care or calmness to the body. Coming to know it and how it is, offering it kindness and care, calming the body.

We have been taking this time with concentration practice and then connecting to the body. Now, asking yourself, "Is the body open? If not, why not?" Coming to know it a little better right now and whether it is open or closed. And if it is closed, what are the root causes of that?

Now shifting to connecting to emotions. The first invitation is to notice joy or to foster joy. We can always stay connected to the anchor point of the breath, body, or sound. In many ways, there can be joy present in our lives. If it's not obvious, we can look for it. Can there be joy just in knowing that you have sight, if you have sight? Or that you have hearing, if you have hearing? Or can there be joy in this breath of air that is relatively clean and is nourishing your body? Inviting elements in of joy right now. We are fostering the part of the mind and heart that nurtures joy right now.

What is in your life that brings joy, if there are elements that bring joy? Just noticing that.

What is bringing you joy in this moment, if there are elements that are bringing you joy now?

Now, while being connected with your anchor of breath, body, or sound, inviting in happiness, if you like. Fostering happiness. Noticing what brings happiness in your life. Looking for it. If it's not so obvious, can it be the clear blue sky or the smile of child? Connecting with a loved one? Doing well on a school project or completing an important project at work? What brings happiness, and can we actually foster happiness in the heart in this moment? It's like we are at the gym right now, working out our muscles, here we are working out our heart—the regions that foster joy and happiness.

The next invitation is to start to bring awareness to the emotional tone. We were just fostering joy and happiness, but now we are invited to open up to see what feelings are here in this moment.

Are they steady, or are they shifting?

We always have that anchor point of the breath, body, or sound to come back to. Connecting in with our emotions, or our heart.

While staying anchored as we need to, inviting ourselves to calm our emotions and to offer kindness toward them, if we choose, which may come in the form of compassion toward our emotions or friendly kindness toward our emotions. Being there with them and allowing them to be calmed and cared for.

Then as you are ready, if you like, just connecting in with the heart, and asking:

Is my heart open?

If not, why not?

If there are elements that are causing the heart to be closed, just observing those with kindness, friendliness, and curiosity. Offering self-care as we explore anything that may be constricting the heart.

Being there with the calmness of those emotions or caring for those emotions, including the reasons why the heart might be more closed, if it is closed. In time, as we have cared for the emotions, seeing the roots of why the heart is closed.

As we are there with the roots and are exploring the root of the heart being closed in any way, seeing if any insights arise around skillful next steps.

What would be a wise and maybe even a courageous next step to care for the roots of why the heart may be closed, to care for them, and allow the heart to open?

An open heart is a wonderful thing. So, maybe there is a skillful next step that will allow for that opening of the heart and the wonderful emotions that come with it, if you feel like that is something you would like to do.

Always respecting your limits and staying within your comfort zone or growth zone.

If you find yourself in the overwhelmed zone, just coming back to that anchor point of the breath, body, or sound. Not needing to push anything or force anything.

Just allowing the heart to gently open like a flower would slowly open in springtime. It takes its time, but it's so beautiful in so many ways because it does take its time to open. .

And then as you are ready, inviting the awareness to return to your anchor point, of the breath, the palms of the hands, the soles of the feet, or sound. Narrowing your focus again to work on that attention right there with the background in place of the breath, body, or sound.

As you are ready, inviting the eyes to open as this meditation starts to come toward a close. Inviting you to physically stretch if that would be beneficial to you. And allowing you to continue on with the next section of the book or the next part of your day.

We can find moments of awakening, or openness. As we learn what leads to our heart openings and closings, we can deliberately scale up in our lives what leads to an open heart and scale down what closes it. Over time, that will lead to spending more time with an open heart and being emotionally well, which leads to flourishing. In my communications with Jon Kabat-Zinn (2021) during writing this book, he shared how moments of awakening can be strung together: "Moments of awakening are continually available to us and can be strung together simply by sustaining awareness as best we can, especially when anchored in the body as a whole, along with the sensations of breathing. The term 'awakening' points to this possibility because it suggests a dynamic process that is always here, always available, realizable in the only moment we ever have—this one." In the next chapter, we will turn to opening the mind, or in other words, working with our thoughts and freeing them.

Home Practices

1. Take a moment to reflect on the intention for the week that you made at the end of chapter 1. How did it go completing that intention? Notice with curiosity and without judgment, seeing

what arises in your thoughts and emotions around how you met or didn't meet the goal that you set. I invite you to set an intention for this coming week using the home practice #1 reflection at the end of chapter 1, but instead apply it to you in this moment in time. You might like to either continue with the intention from last time or set a new one related to opening the heart or caring for your emotions. What arises naturally within you that feels like your true self wanting to express? Those are often the best intentions, as what arises naturally is just you being you.

2. With the focus on developing your attention control, I invite you to do an attentional focus mindfulness practice every day, such as the first meditation offered in chapter 1.

3. Every other day this week, I invite you to work with your choice of contemplations from this chapter, depending what which ones resonate with you, specifically: (1) loving-kindness meditation, (2) the first eight contemplations in the Discourse on Breathing Mindfulness (which are summarized in appendix 2 if you'd like to see them in one place), (3) the contemplation on opening the heart, or (4) the STOP practice. In doing them, I encourage you to notice how your day goes afterward, so you come to know if and how each one supports you, giving you feedback that can continue to support and motivate you to practice in ways that care for your emotions and support your emotional regulation.

CHAPTER 3

Opening the Mind
Clarity and Flourishing

Jackson, at the age of eighteen, took a gap year after high school to travel. He went to North Korea to compare it with what he heard from the media, books, and other people. As Jackson planned a year of travel, he realized that he wanted to see places relatively untouched by western influences. In the northern region of North Korea, he found nature that looked undisturbed by humans. He also found beauty, such as architectural approaches unlike any he had seen. He got to know his North Korean guides. One evening, they started talking politics, comparing what they had been taught about the history of North Korea. One of the guides was adamant about how the history of his country was like the story of David and Goliath, where North Koreans feel like David against the mighty United States. The guide explained his belief that North Koreans are genuinely peaceful and that North Korea developed nuclear weapons primarily to stay safe by deterring the United States from attacking.

Jackson explored keeping an open mind to it all and allowed wisdom to grow in himself about how societies function. By opening to it all, he could see the whole more clearly, recognizing it is nearly impossible to understand the whole of anything. After his trip Jackson shared, "People there are just looking for happiness, like people are everywhere. We often just hear the political perspective, but don't hear about the people themselves."

Having an open mind maximizes our chances of complete understanding—in other words, wisdom. With Jackson's ability to be aware of his thoughts related to fear or judgment about North Korea that he had heard in the media, he was able to let go of the unhelpful thoughts, act on the useful ones, and learn, with an open mind, about a culture few westerners have visited. This in turn brought him happiness, joy, and wisdom.

That's the topic of this chapter—opening the mind. An awareness of the mind, often referred to as thoughts, is the final corner of the MBSR and MBC triangle (figure 1.2). That awareness of all three elements—sensations, emotions, and thoughts—is in many ways the entire human experience. If we can bring awareness to them, they can become a wedge between the stressor and response, giving us a moment to pause and make a more skillful decision on how to respond (figure 3.1).

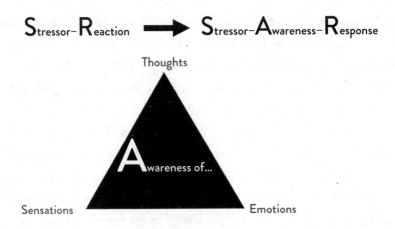

Stressor–**R**eaction ➡ **S**tressor–**A**wareness–**R**esponse

Thoughts

Awareness of...

Sensations   Emotions

Figure 3.1 The triangle of awareness (awareness of physical sensations, emotions, and thoughts) can act as a wedge between a stressor and the immediate *reaction* to it, and instead allow awareness to foster a more considered *response* to that stressor.

This chapter will show you how to be aware of your mind, care for you mind, not take your mental formations too seriously, let go of ones that are not helpful, and direct the mind toward those that are. The chapter is organized around the next four contemplations in the Discourse on Breathing Mindfulness, which are focused on the mind, or *citta* in Pāli. In

English, *citta* can be translated as the heart-mind-consciousness complex that is basically involved in thinking (Buddhadāsa Bhikkhu 1988). When *citta* is reduced to one English word, "mind" is what I most often see.

I will share some contemplations to help you become more aware of your mind in a nonjudgmental way (the ninth contemplation), how to direct your mind toward thoughts that are productive and promote happiness (the tenth contemplation), how to concentrate your mind (the eleventh contemplation), and how to liberate it (the twelfth contemplation). In doing so, you can be freer of limiting conditions, such as jealousy, anxiety, and anger, and instead dwell more in joy, happiness, and well-being.

DISCOURSE ON BREATHING MINDFULNESS:
Third Tetrad of Contemplations

9. Breathing in, I am aware of my mind (citta). Breathing out, I am aware of my mind.

10. Breathing in, I gladden my mind. Breathing out, I gladden my mind.

11. Breathing in, I concentrate my mind. Breathing out, I concentrate my mind.

12. Breathing in, I liberate my mind. Breathing out, I liberate my mind.

Aware of the Mind

DISCOURSE ON BREATHING MINDFULNESS:
Ninth Contemplation

9. Breathing in, I am aware of my mind. Breathing out, I am aware of my mind.

Being aware of our mind, or what our heart-mind-conscious complex, is sharing with us, can help us see who we really are. It can identify what our mind deeply wants in order to be happier and live a fuller life. Brady's story is a brief example.

Brady, an undergraduate student who went through the Meditation, Mindfulness, and Health course, shared that he had always been focused on a premed lifestyle. He went through high school knowing what he needed to get done, such as getting a high GPA and research experience. During the first two years of college, he was on autopilot mode. For example, he thought to himself, *I don't have a leadership role yet. I should apply to something. I should do it just to say I have experience.* During his freshman and sophomore years, he didn't use the shopping period to explore different courses; instead, he just put in required classes and didn't think too much about what electives he wanted to take.

However, during the semester he went through mindfulness training, he had more time for introspective thought. He shared, "I have a better understanding of who I am. It's helping me know what I want to do besides just getting into med school. If I don't have another hobby besides schoolwork, I won't have anything to do. I am realizing I have wanted to skateboard since elementary school. I gave up on it because my friends didn't really do it and my neighborhood wasn't great for it (very hilly). Mindfulness has helped me understand what I want to do besides school." This awareness of his thoughts was showing him who he really was and led him down the path of living a fuller life.

You can think of the first three chapters of this book as the making of a three-point inspection of sorts: the body (chapter 1), heart (chapter 2), and mind (chapter 3). Of course, a major domain of the mind is thoughts. Even in this moment, I invite you to notice where your thoughts are. Your thoughts are different from anyone else's thoughts. That is the unique beauty in each of us (even if some of our thoughts are less than beautiful).

Open monitoring refers to the practice of paying attention to our physical sensations, emotions, and thoughts. Pretty much the entire human experience is through these three domains. Open monitoring meditation trains us to disentangle our experiences so we can better understand them in these three categories: sensations, emotions, and thoughts. Through better understanding them, we can take wiser action on the important messages they provide. The meditation is offered below.

Open Monitoring Meditation

The intention of this meditation is to train ourselves in self-awareness of our physical sensations, thoughts, and emotions. In doing so, we can be more sensitive to understanding the messages they provide to us. Through this knowledge, we can respond to take greater advantage of every situation that arises in real time. We can harness the clues that come from these sense domains to create a life that best matches our environment, who we are, and our natural skills and passions because we better understand what they are.

Inviting you to settle into a posture for meditation that fosters comfort and alertness.

Finding your way to your anchor point of the breath or a particular part of the body, like the palms of the hands or the soles of the feet, or the raw sensations of sound. For most of us, it will be the breath, if we are comfortable with that.

Allowing the concentration to be right here, right now, with the chosen object of meditation: the breath, body, or sound.

As thoughts or feelings arise, just noticing them, exploring them a little bit, and letting them go. Coming back to this moment and to this breath, this part of the body, or this sound.

The next invitation is to widen the aperture of awareness to now include the body, if you haven't already been doing that, and particularly focusing on the parts of the body that are in contact with the surface you are resting on. Taking a moment to notice sensations of the feet on the ground or the sit bones on the surface that you are sitting on, for example.

Then continuing to widen awareness to encompass the entire body.

So here we are observing the body.

It's kind of like sitting on the bank of a river watching a leaf floating by.

The leaf may get caught in ebbs and flows of the river or into little whirlpools, and we are sitting on the riverbank just observing it.

So what's here in the body right now?

Are there particular parts of the body that are speaking more loudly than others, and what messages do they have around comfort or discomfort, or warmth or coolness, or touch? Just taking some time to monitor the sensations in the body moment by moment.

And then if you like, starting to shift awareness to the sensation of sound. And here we are with those raw elements of sound, like the pitch (how high or low it is), the volume (how loud or soft it is), whether it's rhythmic or arrhythmic, and its location.

Taking some time to be there with the raw elements. Noticing when we give meaning to the sound (for example identifying the sound as someone walking by or as a plane flying above), and seeing if we can let go of that meaning and just be there with the raw elements of sound itself.

Each time the mind wanders, just noticing that, knowing it's okay. It's what the mind does. Inviting it back with gentleness, firmness, and kindness to the object of meditation, which in this case is sound or lack of sound.

The next invitation, if you like, is to start to connect to the sensation of emotion, or feeling tones. Just noticing what is being sensed here. Are the emotions positive, neutral, or negative? Or even naming a specific emotion that is present right now, maybe it is peacefulness or agitation.

Just noticing those emotions as they shift and change moment to moment, or if there is steadiness to the emotions, noticing that.

Now inviting the mind to go into the domain of thoughts. Starting to observe those thought patterns, like clouds floating by in a clear blue sky.

We are just watching those thoughts pass along.

Observing the thoughts shift and change, and if there is space between the thoughts, noticing that.

All the while we are sitting, not getting too engaged with those thoughts—they are just thoughts—but observing them.

And now, if you like, taking some time to observe what is arising in the physical sensations, emotions, and thoughts as a whole. Instead of focusing in on just one of these areas, can you be open to them all, noticing what arises, moment to moment? Perhaps it will be a sensation in your leg for example, that will lead to a thought, followed by an emotion. Training yourself to be here now with this entire experience of being alive, knowing that you can always return to your anchor point if you need to get settled.

And then as this meditation starts to come toward a close, returning to your anchor point. For many of us it's the breath, but for some it's an object of the body, like the palms of the hands or the soles of the feet, or sound.

Returning back to that anchor and staying with that anchor point as long as you like, as this meditation comes to a close.

Part of this meditation is to invite you to know through connecting with the physical sensations, emotions, and thoughts (the triangle of awareness shown in figure 1.2), how and who you are today. In knowing with clarity where we are at, we can embrace it and move forward with fuller wisdom on how to navigate the river that our raft is on here and now. Toward the end, this meditation invites us to observe our thoughts. Part of observing our thoughts is coming to know when they are helpful or not and also that they are just thoughts that we don't necessarily need to act on.

Often, with thoughts in the mind, they can pile on and create more injury than the original cause of hurt. It's like we have been shot with an arrow, but then our thoughts are like second, third, and fourth arrows going into the same wound, making it worse. For example, in response to getting cut off in traffic, we might yell at the driver, who yells back at us, we might then ruminate on it, then regret yelling at the driver, but at the same time we want to retaliate and imagine all the ways we could retaliate, and so on. All these thoughts are like other arrows hitting the wound. Part of practicing awareness of our thoughts is noticing if they are helpful in this moment, and if they aren't, letting them go so we can focus on what brings us and other happiness and fulfillment. Indeed, the final part of the meditation above, where we return to our anchor point, is training us to let go of observing the thoughts, return to this moment, and direct the mind toward the next object of attention.

One day after teaching, I was walking across the street in the middle of the crosswalk, and a car turned and came toward me. I saw it and started to step backward looking for the best way to get out of the way. I was squarely in the middle so couldn't easily go to one side or the other. As the car came at me, I placed my hand on the hood and got ready to jump up on it. Through the windshield, I could see an older woman on the passenger side with wide eyes yelling at her husband in the driver's seat. He slammed on the brakes. I noticed my thought, *This guy almost ended my ability to take care of my daughters*. I could feel the energy and anger rising in me. I walked directly over to his window and saw his face. He looked terrible—shocked and upset. I could feel compassion arising in me and noticed a thought that yelling at him wasn't going to help. I said to him, "It's okay," and continued walking.

Awareness of my thoughts in that moment not only helped me physically respond to the car, but also helped not make it worse for the driver, his wife, or me by yelling at him. If I had yelled, it wouldn't have helped him, I suspect, as it looked like he already felt terrible. I also probably would have regretted yelling at him, knowing that would probably have hurt him and caused me to lose my own groundedness. That regret would have been like more arrows being shot into the wound of nearly getting hit by the car. My yelling would have added more wounds to the driver. By being aware of my thoughts and letting go of the unhelpful ones, the experience became one of learning about my thoughts in that moment and trusting and appreciating the response. This incident reminded me that practicing observing our thoughts, emotions, and physical sensations can literally save our lives and provide a happier, healthy life. Indeed, making the mind happier, or gladdening the mind, is the topic of the next section.

Gladdening the Mind

DISCOURSE ON BREATHING MINDFULNESS:
Tenth Contemplation

10. *Breathing in, I gladden my mind. Breathing out, I gladden my mind.*

Another translation of this contemplation is "Breathing in, I make my mind happy. Breathing out, I make my mind happy" (Nhat Hanh 2008).

After having worked with this contemplation for twenty years, I find it allows me to connect with my true self and the world around me better. It fosters my ability to move toward the positive elements in my life that are sitting right there in front of me but that I often don't let in or fully appreciate. It also encourages me to let go of persistent negative ruminations that aren't serving me or others and instead direct my thoughts to more fruitful places, leading me to be happier and serve others better. As I mentioned earlier, evidence suggests that this is one of the ways that mindfulness-based programs work. Specifically, a systematic review and meta-analysis of eight clinical trials showed that reducing repetitive negative thinking is a mechanism by which mindfulness training improves mental health (Gu et al. 2015). The following story is a case in point.

This tale, inspired by an ancient Zen story (for example, Muth 2005), is about two young monks, called Brother Due and Brother Giang, who were walking along a path through the forest. They were on their way to a palace to celebrate the queen's birthday. They came up to a lovely wide river and decided to take a rest along the riverbank. The two men enjoyed the coolness of the breeze coming off the river and dipped their feet in the water, enjoying the sensations of it flowing around their ankles and toes. A wealthy lady named Cara arrived at the river in a carriage pulled by horses. The horses stalled, not wanting to cross the moving water. The driver yelled at the horses, cracking his whip, and they haltingly moved forward into the water. The horses got part way across the river, and the carriage became stuck. Cara scowled as she looked out the window and started scolding the driver for getting them trapped. The driver got down out of the seat and tried to tug the horses across the river. The wagon was too heavy to be pulled through the water and over the river rocks. They were wedged.

Brother Due walked into the river and offered to carry Cara across on his back while the driver managed the scared horses. She exclaimed with a grumpy "hmph!" but nonetheless climbed onto his back. He carefully carried her across the river and placed her on the far shore. She got down, and immediately checked her clothes to make sure they hadn't gotten damaged. Brother Due then went back to the carriage, and with Brother Giang, started to unload some of the bags and boxes to carry across while the carriage driver tried to steady the horses. When they had lightened the load enough, the horses were able to pull the carriage across the river and up onto the riverbank to safety.

Brother Due looked kindly toward the well-dressed lady, and she was engrossed in telling the driver how incompetent he was and how they had almost gotten hurt. She ignored the young men who had helped.

The two monks continued their way down the forest path toward the castle to celebrate the queen's birthday. The path was quiet, except for occasional birds chirping, and the sound of the gentle wind rustling through the treetops. After some time, Brother Giang said to Brother Due, "I can't believe that lady didn't thank you for carrying her across the river! You saved her from a great deal of hardship." Due looked at Giang, with his eyes gently easing into a smile, and said, "Dear friend, I put her down hours ago. Why are you still carrying her?"

Mindfulness training can help with the self-awareness (figure 1.1) to notice that we are engaged in repetitive negative thinking and ask ourselves, "Is it helpful for my mind to be here right now?" If yes, then continue with your mind there; if not, then you can utilize your meditation-training-enhanced attention control to bank out of that negative spiral of thoughts and actually place your mind where it would be of most service now. That may well be on a happier thought.

Let's try out this contemplation to see how it feels for you. Keep in mind that with this contemplation, and any in this book, you can always let it go if you find after trying it out that it doesn't serve you or others well.

Gladding the Mind Meditation

The intention of this meditation is to gladden the mind, or make it happier. Often our thoughts and emotions are swirling in the negative domain, such as identifying real or possible problems and how to fix them, which is fine if that is where the mind needs to be. Often though, the body, heart, and mind operate better in a more neutral or positive space. In many ways we are alive because our ancestors were constantly monitoring for negative events, such as predators, avoiding food shortages, and ensuring shelter against the elements. Our bodies are set up biologically to monitor for negative events, which is important and promotes survival. It doesn't necessary support happiness and flourishing though, and sometimes training the mind to be able to dwell in a happier place can set us up for greater well-being, thereby improving our ability to better serve others through our enhanced well-being and resilience.

Remembering that usually the sixteen contemplations in this discourse are done in one sitting (and you are welcome to offer yourself the prior ones at any time, including now), inviting you to check in with your anchor point of the breath, body, or sound. Spending a little time settling in, with this grounding object of meditation, letting the concentration be just with it, and if the attention wanders, inviting it back with kindness.

Checking in with the body (physical sensations) and heart (emotions), and perhaps asking are they open? If not, why not?

Starting to bring awareness now to the mind and particularly to the thoughts. Seeing what's here in the thoughts right now, observing them like an unbiased scientist would observe data coming in. Noticing what thoughts are arising and holding them with kindness and without any judgment.

Now inviting you to offer yourself the contemplation:

Connecting to my anchor point such as the breath, I make my mind happier. Gladdening my mind. Noticing what thoughts are here and considering ones that bring happiness. Perhaps being like a chef in a kitchen who is selecting ingredients to add a particular flavor in the food, such as savory, sweet, or rich. As a chef of your mind, working with your self-awareness, attention control, and emotion regulation, can you foster thoughts that result in the "taste" of gladdening the mind, even just for this brief moment?

Returning to your anchor point, as this meditation transitions to a close, inviting you to notice if and how it informs this next phase of your day.

Concentrating the Mind

DISCOURSE ON BREATHING MINDFULNESS:
Eleventh Contemplation

11. *Breathing in, I concentrate my mind. Breathing out, I concentrate my mind.*

Concentration is fundamental to insight. In fact, in Buddhism there is a trifecta, which is mindfulness plus concentration leads to insight. If the first two are strong, we are more likely to get to the last one. It's one thing to be aware of our thoughts, and it's another to be able to direct the thoughts where we want them to go and keep them there to get whatever job done that our mindful awareness indicates is necessary, knowing that sometimes that job is just to be fully present.

If our *mindful awareness* is so sensitive that we know exactly what is experienced in our body and mind in a nonjudgmental, curious, gentle way, and we *concentrate* the mind to be there with the experience, insights are more free to arise. Once the insights arise, mindfulness and concentration are a dynamic duo that support us in acting on those insights. Specifically, our ability to concentrate keeps us focused on taking the wise next steps without distraction (such as being carried off by a notification that just popped up on our phone). Our mindful awareness of thoughts, emotions, and sensations helps remind us how important that next step is, give us the feedback on how it's going in completing it, and indicate if we need to shift directions based on the reality that is unfolding step-by-step as we engage in this next important phase of life.

Alexa is a squash player who went through one of my mindfulness programs. She shared that in her junior year of high school, she saw a sports psychologist. The psychologist helped guide her in some mindfulness meditations, which planted the first seeds that made her aware of the connection between sports and mindfulness. Now that she plays squash at the college level, one of her biggest issues has been her focus and how easily she gets distracted. Alexa shared that even though she is at the court in person, she often feels she is not there mentally. She found that mindfulness training changed her approach to distraction during games. The "one point at a time" strategy helped her improve her performance on the court. She learned to not think about a past or future point—and instead to focus on just this point now. Having an anchor, such as the breath or a visual mark on the wall to come back to, allowed her to ground herself and reset. This helped to clear her mind, especially between points. She could then attend to the present point and fully play it.

Mindfulness training also helped Alexa enjoy the game more. It's more fun when she's focused. Furthermore, she's seen that sports help her clear her mind to get into a better mental space. With Alexa's improved self-awareness of her thoughts and emotions, she realized how squash is a good way to meet interesting people and that when she plays regularly, she is happier and healthier, both mentally and physically.

As Alexa's story indicates, mindfulness can help develop concentration. One of the most fundamental exercises to do so is meditating on the breath or another anchor point, which is what we have been doing in all the contemplations so far. Many mindfulness traditions begin with counting the breath. For example, with an in-breath, count "one," and the next breath, count "two," all the way up to ten. Once you reach a count of ten breaths, start back at one. If your mind wanders, which it will, just notice where it went. That is good information about yourself today and where you mind is dwelling. Then with gentleness and firmness, bring it back to the breath, starting back at number one. If it's tough to keep the mind on the breath because it's so busy, you are not alone. In fact, you are probably in the company of just about everybody reading this book.

One anchor point can be to place your hand on your diaphragm so you can feel the up and down of the belly and chest as you breathe. Try counting in this way. Over time, if this practice resonates with you, you will get better at it, and it will get easier. In doing so, your ability to concentrate will be enhanced. You may find yourself concentrating better on your schoolwork or on what your loved one is sharing with you. You may find yourself more in the zone during that athletic event when it matters most or feeling the flow of artistic expression flow through your hands and onto the paper or screen in your design work. It can show up in lots of ways.

If breathing for you is not a comfortable place (for example if you have asthma or had a traumatic event related to your breathing), it's okay to use a different anchor point here too. As with the previous practices, you can use the body, such as the palms of the hands or soles of the feet, or even sound.

Indeed, every mindfulness exercise I have offered so far should train your concentration, but some are more effective than others. As you play around with the different exercises, I invite you to see which ones develop your concentration more. Concentration plus mindfulness equals insight. Insight leads to a happier, healthier, more productive life. Now all that's left is to free the mind.

Liberating the Mind

DISCOURSE ON BREATHING MINDFULNESS:
Twelfth Contemplation

12. Breathing in, I liberate my mind. Breathing out, I liberate my mind.

I love this contemplation. Liberating or freeing the mind means releasing it from any mental formations that are causing unnecessary suffering. For example, it could be releasing thoughts that are leading you down an unhelpful path, releasing fears of being judged by others, releasing yourself from craving a career path that won't actually bring net happiness, or perhaps releasing attachment to a material item that causes more harm than benefit.

There is a story of the Buddha in a grove in the forest, teaching his monks, when a farmer came running into the grove and yelled, "Excuse me, I'm sorry to bother you, but my cows have run away! Have you seen them?" The Buddha responded that he hadn't, and after the farmer ran off to look in another direction, the Buddhas shared with his monks, "Aren't you glad that you don't have any cows?"

What cows can you let go of? Do you have thoughts about what you or others "should" be doing, such as working eighty-hour weeks even if you don't feel it is healthy for you to do so, becoming a doctor even though you don't really want to, vaping that thing because some of your friends do, or being worried about other people judging you for who you are? Well, can you let that go and just be yourself? If you do that, chances are high that things will work out just fine—that you will find a career that you are good at because you are doing what you love in ways that help others; that you will find a romantic partner who is a good fit because you are who you are, which makes you easier to understand and relate to.

Cole, who went through MBC, shared, "I think it's definitely helping me be integrated more conspicuously and tangibly in this final exam period. I have never been healthier than in the past five days. My smartwatch is buzzing once every day, showing I achieved my physical activity goal. I am getting more exercise than I have before. I know that I am being good to myself in that way and watching myself eating better, finding more time, meditating, and doing some yoga. When I have a spare minute, even though it's getting harder and harder to find as finals get closer and closer, I'll read or play some guitar. I played tennis the other day, which I hadn't done that all semester, and it was wonderful. A lot of my friends are in bad places right now mentally, but I am very happy, even though I have finals coming up."

Cole freed his mind from notions about it being necessary to suffer during the exam period, and instead followed his body's, heart's, and mind's messages to take care of himself, even doing things like playing guitar or tennis that filled him up efficiently, that normally he or his friends wouldn't do during the exam period. What is your body, mind, and heart telling you, that you can trust, that liberates your mind? I invite you to put down this book (assuming the messages do not involve reading it), and do it right now. What is your freed-up mind sharing would be a wise next step for you to do in this moment?

Deep Relaxation

One of the practices that our research showed that was among the most appreciated adaptations for young adults was the deep relaxation meditation (Loucks et al. 2021). I don't know about you, but a lot of people feel stressed and often have trouble sleeping. Deep relaxation is designed to allow us to let go of our swirling thoughts and instead direct them toward our body, with a focus on appreciating each and every part of the body, as well as relaxing it. It is grounded in a deep relaxation meditation that Thich Nhat Hanh has offered (Nhat Hanh 2007).

Let's go through it together in the guided meditation below. If you prefer to listen to it (which maybe better, given it is about relaxing and maybe even sleeping), you can also find the recording on the website for this book, http://www.newharbinger.com/49135. If now isn't a good time to try it out, I invite you to read the practice below so you understand it and then practice it at a time you feel it would be helpful, such as when you go to bed at night.

Deep Relaxation Meditation

The deep relaxation practice starts like the body scan, where the invitation is to lie down in a restful place, like your bed, couch, yoga mat, or rug. Unlike the body scan, where the invitation is to fall awake, in deep relaxation, you are invited to fall asleep, if that feels helpful to you—although remaining awake is also fine. Many people use this meditation to help them sleep at night. Another distinction of how the deep relaxation practice is different is that with the body scan, you are invited to explore each part of the body with curiosity to develop deeper understanding of how it is in this moment, thereby understanding yourself more and increasing body awareness. The deep relaxation practice is consistent with this approach but adds two unique elements: First, the deep relaxation practice offers gratitude and loving-kindness to the part of the body being contemplated. Second, the invitation is to deliberately relax that part of the body—to let any tension in it go. Similarly with any meditation, as you notice your thoughts arise, if they are outside of your contemplation of that part of the body, then the invitation is to note the thoughts and then let them go, returning your attention back to the part or the body that is the object of meditation. So let's get started.

Inviting you to take a moment and settle into a position that is comfortable for a deep relaxation meditation.

Finding your way probably onto your back, with the arms resting by the sides of the body and the legs straight, unless having the legs up on a chair in astronaut pose would be better for your back.

Coming to feel the body where it is in contact with the surface you are lying on, such as the backs of the shoulders, hips, legs, heels, and hands.

Coming to be with the entire body and noticing how it is feeling in this moment.

What is here?

Recognizing that as we go through this practice, if any parts of the body do not feel safe to be with, maybe due to a traumatic memory or a current injury, then to just let the contemplation on that body part go for now, returning back to your anchor, such as the breath, a different particular part of the body (like the hands or feet), or the sensation of sound, or just skipping that part of the body and moving onto the next one.

Then in the future, if or when you are a ready, venturing out to be with that part of the body if it is in your comfort or growth zone but not if it is in the overwhelmed zone.

Spending some time in this position, being here with the body.

As you are ready, inviting you to start to muscularly tense the entire body.

Creating clenched fists, tensing the muscles in the arms, contracting the shoulder muscles and the muscles in the neck and face, continuing to engage all muscles in the body including the chest, back, abdominal muscles, as well as the muscles in the legs and feet.

Contracting and tensing every muscle in the body.

Holding it, noticing how that feels, still holding, and then...

Letting the muscle tension go.

Releasing that tension, and noticing the physical sensations, feelings, and thoughts as the release in tension unfolds.

Being there with it, letting it be just as it is.

As you are ready, starting to bring awareness down through the left leg and into the left foot, noticing what is here in the left big toe, just like you would with the body scan.

Now, however, you are invited to offer some gratitude to the left big toe. (I know, it's a little weird.)

If you have ever hurt it, you know how important that strong toe is for walking around each day, for doing what is needed and what brings you joy in your life.

Offering some gratitude to the left big toe, and as you are ready, letting it relax.

Giving that toe the rest it needs and that it deserves.

Shifting attention over to the smaller toes in the left foot, remembering that each provides stability and mobility, and thanking them for what they do.

Offering them some deliberate relaxation in this moment.

Now shifting awareness into the sole of the left foot, aware of all the tendons, ligaments, bones, and muscles that allow you to move throughout your day.

Even if they are less than perfectly healthy, appreciating them for what they do provide.

Coming to know them just a little more in this moment, and offering them kindness and rest as you deliberately relax the sole of the left foot.

Moving awareness along the foot to the Achilles tendon that connects the heel to the leg and without which you couldn't walk.

Offering loving-kindness and gratitude to this part of the body and how it allows you to move and to serve others.

Offering this part of the body an opportunity to not only feel appreciated but to rest.

Letting go any tension in the Achilles tendon.

And in this way, I invite you to move through the entire body, exploring it at your own pace and offering loving-kindness, gratitude, relaxation, and rest to each and every part of the body that serves you and others so well.

Remembering, if you are breathing, there is more right with you than wrong with you.

While your body may be imperfect, as all of ours are, it is also in many ways perfect.

The body is a remarkable society of cells working to support you and others in this moment of life.

I invite you to spend some time with this practice, coming to know each and every part just a little better, offering it gratitude for what it does, and giving it well-deserved rest and relaxation.

As the thoughts float over to other topics, just noticing that, and without any judgment and with kindness and firmness, bringing the awareness back to the body part that you are focusing on, giving that part your kind attention, knowing that you are here for it, and offering it thankfulness and rest.

Toward the end of the meditation, the invitation is to hold the entire body in awareness, offering gratitude to it for what it does to support your and others' lives, and to give it this well-deserved moment of rest.

Snnorrrrre.....

Well, I hope you had a good nap and didn't drool on this book.

This practice is a way to shape our thoughts toward gratitude and groundedness in the body, opening the mind to its connection with the body, and letting the body and mind have the rest they deserve so they are there to serve you and others better.

Letting Go of Hindrances

As we look for ways to open the mind, one of them is to let go of judging things as good or bad. They just are the way they are. Can we let go of the temptation to fuss about them?

There is a classic Taoist story about a farmer who lived in a productive and beautiful valley, planting and harvesting vegetable crops (for example, Muth 2005). It was hard work but fulfilling. The work was made easier by having a strong pair of horses to put his plow and a capable son to work with.

One evening, someone mistakenly left the gate to the horse corral open. One of the horses let herself out and vanished into the countryside. Upon hearing the news of the horse's disappearance, the farmer's neighbors exclaimed, "That is terrible! What a loss. It's not fair that happened." The farmer looked at them, smiled, and gently said, "Maybe."

A couple of days later, the horse returned. Alongside her were two wild horses she had attracted. The wild horses came into the corral, and the farmer found them all out there one morning eating food he had left out for his missing horse in case she returned. The neighbors saw what had happened and joyously came over to celebrate the good news. "How wonderful!" they exclaimed. "It's amazing that not only your horse returned, but she brought two more with her! What good luck!" The farmer grinned, as he too was happy, but upon reflecting a little more said, "Perhaps."

Over the next week, the farmer's son began to break the wild horses. He would enter the corral with them and slowly and gently allow them to get used to him. He fed them, talking kindly and softly. Over time, the son began to ride them. During a riding session, one of the wild horses bucked him off, and he fell through the air landing on a fence beam, breaking his leg. The neighbors learned of this news and shared how sorry they were that it had happened. "What bad luck," they said. "That shouldn't have been. It's not fair that such a kind young man is so injured, especially as you are preparing for the harvest season." "Maybe," the farmer responded with a sad but gentle smile.

The next day, the army came through enlisting the young who were capable of fighting in an ongoing war with a neighboring nation. Seeing the son with a broken leg, they passed him by, allowing him to stay on the farm. The neighbors could not believe this luck and expressed their delight and how wonderful it was that the son did not need to go to war. The farmer once again, with his eyes smiling and creased, said, "Maybe."

This idea of freeing the mind of anything hindering, including judgments about whether something is "good" or "bad," is a rich area for contemplation and growth. So that leads us to one of the fundamental contemplations of this chapter, which is the meditation on opening the mind.

Opening the Mind Meditation

The intention of this meditation is to first ground ourselves in the body and the heart and then to explore into the mind to see if it is open, or in other words, liberated from any thoughts or other mental formations that are causing agitation. If the mind is clenched, agitated, or in other words, closed, we explore the roots of that in this meditation and create space for wise next steps to appear once we understand what is causing the mind to close. In doing so, it can allow us to foster a finely tuned mind, that is coupled with a finely tuned body and heart, to unleash our remarkable potential within. In this way, we can be healthier and happier, help others be healthier and happier, and take action on our calling.

> *The invitation first is to guide yourself in a meditation that starts on your anchor point (such as the breath, body, or sound), and spend some time there developing your concentration.*
>
> *Then, as you are ready, bringing awareness to physical sensations, in other words, the body. Spending some time with the body, noticing the sensations arising, shifting, changing, and perhaps fading away,*

replaced by other sensations. If some physical sensations are steady, noticing that steadiness.

Asking yourself as you are ready, "Is my body open? If not, why not?"

Being with any closures of the body (for example, an overly full stomach or a feeling of lethargy from not exercising) in a kind way, caring for them. If and as you are ready, exploring the roots of any closures in the body, with kindness and curiosity.

Shifting next to asking, "Is my heart open? If not, why not?" Using similar practices as above for the body to be with any closures if they are there (such as feeling shut down toward someone emotionally), and exploring their roots, seeing if you can release yourself, even just a little bit, from any hindrances that are causing your heart to be more closed.

And then, asking yourself, "Is my mind open?" (Or you may want to try, "Is my mind free?") If not, why not?

If your mind isn't open (for example by having racing out-of-control thoughts or feeling overly closed to a family member's ideas), can you care for that closed mind with kindness and understanding that it is just the way the mind is in this moment and it's okay? Then, in time, inviting you to look for the roots of the knot that is causing your mind to be less open, that is causing you to suffer. And, like a sailor who is skilled at tying and untying knots, inviting you to loosen that knot and as a result let your mind be freer.

You might like to close this meditation by returning to your anchor point of the breath, body, or sound to ground back in, focusing attention on this familiar safe place, and then as you are ready, opening the eyes and bringing this version of yourself to the next step in your day.

When the mind is completely open and partnered with an open body and an open heart, we have built the foundation for nothing short of an awakening, or what in Buddhist terms is known as enlightenment. In my understanding and experience, the only thing else needed is an open spirit, which is covered in the next chapter.

Home Practice

1. Take a moment to reflect on the intention for the week that you made at the end of chapter 2. How did it go completing that intention? Notice with curiosity and without any judgment, and see what arises in your thoughts and emotions around how you met or didn't meet your goal. If you like, set an intention for this coming week using the "Assess Your Baseline Well-Being" exercise at the end of chapter 1. You might like to either continue with the intention from last time or set a new one related to opening the mind. What arises naturally within you that feels like your true self wanting to express out? Those are often the best intentions, as what naturally arises is just you being you.

2. With the focus on developing your attention control, I invite you to do an attentional focus mindfulness practice every day, maybe even starting your meditations with it, and then shifting to more open monitoring, such as with the practices below.

3. Every other day this week, I invite you to work with your choice of (1) sitting meditation with open monitoring; (2) contemplation on opening the body, heart, and mind; or (3) first twelve contemplations of the Discourse on Breathing Mindfulness (See appendix 2 for the first twelve contemplations in one place). See what arises for you in doing these practices and if you can wisely act on what arises.

4. For several days, try the deep relaxation meditation before you go to sleep at night or at another time that feels appropriate.

CHAPTER 4

Opening the Spirit
Seeing the Big Picture

When my twin daughters were six years old, I felt the need for a solo weeklong retreat. I am committed to be a present, loving father, so I am discerning when it comes to being away from my family. Deep inside, I knew there was something that needed to be explored and let out and that I'd be a better father and husband afterward. I talked with my wife Betsy, and she, as always, supported me in doing this. She knows who I am and that I am a more skillful partner because of my practice. I found a campground in the Catskill Mountains with a campsite in the woods. I packed simple foods to last several days, a meditation cushion, and a big tent that I could meditate in to avoid insects if needed. It was near my root tradition's monastery, Blue Cliff, which I was scheduled to transition to after four solo days to be in community but mostly in silence. I got to the campsite, set up camp, and meditated regularly. In order to create conditions for physical and mental well-being, similar to chapter 1 on opening the body, I walked, jogged, stretched, and ate healthily.

The biggest insight I had on day one was how noisy chipmunks can be when there are a lot of them and they aren't afraid of the meditator sitting among them for hours. Wahoo. By day two in the afternoon, I was feeling frustrated and growing angry. I was getting nothing. No insight. Just sitting here while my wife took care of our children. What was I doing here? I was wasting my time. I felt that energy rising in me and began to harness it—harness it into concentrating on right here, right now. What is here in my body? What is here in my mind? Can I open them? Can I open my heart to this frustration and anger? The energy that was welling up inside broke through, and I launched fully into the present moment. Completely there (here). My heart, mind. My body was well exercised from running and doing yoga that day. Bam. That present-moment awareness held for the rest of the day. It was definitely a record, as my prior record of present-moment awareness was probably about ten minutes. I fell asleep that evening, and in the morning when I awoke, it was gone, momentarily.

As I opened my heart, mind, and body, they continued to get more present and were quickly locked in again. I went for a run later that day, completely there with each step, shifting my awareness to the visual field, my heart, body, mind, wherever seemed best. As I leaned into the experience, I tried to consider how I got there and how I could get there again as the retreat transitioned to daily life in society. I asked myself, "Is my body open? If not, why not?" And then took care of what was causing the body to be closed, offering it kindness and understanding, and then in time, seeing if I could transform those roots or knots in ways that allowed the body to open.

Then similarly I asked, "Is my heart open? If not, why not?" And I continued to care for and explore the fundamental causes of any closures that I had personal control over, seeing what messages were there, and then addressing the causes of the closure to allow the heart to naturally open. In finding ways that open the heart, many of the solutions were contemplations in the Discourse on Breathing Mindfulness, including in the second tetrad, which focuses on emotions.

Then I asked: "Is my mind open? If not, why not?" I cared for, explored, and transformed closures in similar ways as for the prior two. "Are all three open?" That's nice. It's still not quite there. What got me the rest of the way? There aren't quite words to describe the process the first time, but the words that get me back there consistently now are, "Is my spirit open? If not, why not?" In finding ways that open the body, heart, mind, and spirit, many of the solutions were in contemplations of the Discourse on Breathing Mindfulness. This opening lasted continuously for two days.

Then as I transitioned to the monastery, I worked to keep it. As I shared the experience with a monk, he talked about how many of the monks and nuns are in that state most of the time, and he forgets sometimes that others aren't. I noticed things that get me into that state, which are meditation, time on my own, and being in nature. At this point, I can now get into that state mostly on demand, but particularly when I am on my own, in nature, or on retreat. It feels in many ways like what I imagine enlightenment to be, which is open, connected, present-moment awareness, and free of suffering and fear. And, as is the case for many of us, fleeting. But it is possible, in our day-to-day lives, to have moments of awakening even if they are not permanent. And it's possible to string such moments together and have them last longer when they occur. I hope this chapter provides you with resources to support that manifesting in you, if you would like it to.

Opening to Your True Self

The Oxford English Dictionary has no fewer than twenty-two definitions of "spirit." In the context of this book, I consider spirit to be the part of us where the emotions and consciousness dwell, in other words, the soul, or our true self. In many ways, I consider it to simply be the forces of nature, such as the molecules, cells, organs, genetic codes, and environmental conditions we have each been exclusively exposed to, coming together to express what they are.

Okay, so how do we open that? How do we become our true selves? How do we let out what is deeply inside, that best expresses who we are and our best contribution to the world? No big deal.

I invite you to consider what opens you to your true self. For some of us it might be prayer or participation in a religious community, being in nature, meditation, creating a beautiful piece of art, a deep conversation with someone you adore, caring for a young child, or an intimate family dinner, to name a few. Opening the spirit is personal and best driven by your inner wisdom. I can only give so many directions here. Nonetheless, below I offer some of the more advanced Buddhist teachings that can open the spirit, that can help you see truth in the way the world works.

If you dabble in these teachings and get snagged, I'd recommend connecting with a knowledgeable person, such as a skilled mindfulness teacher or even a counselor with meditation and mindfulness training. Sometimes it really helps to just talk out challenges you are having with a professional. We also have regular free online live teacher-led mindfulness sessions offered by the Mindfulness Center at Brown that you are welcome to check out (http://brown.edu/mindfulnesscenter).

Also remember that these teachings are offered with the invitation to try them on and not hold them too tightly. If they bring happiness and well-being, then continue on with them. If not, then let them go. Please respect your limits and work in domains that are in your comfort zone or growth zone (figure 2.2) and trust your inner wisdom. Feel free to ignore these teachings and seek out your own sources of opening your spirit. Trust that inner wisdom. Below are a few approaches in case you want to play around with them.

This chapter is organized around the final four contemplations in the Discourse on Breathing Mindfulness (Nhat Hanh 2008). Note that these four contemplations are typically reflected on after the twelve prior contemplations that open the body, heart, and mind. It is only when that base is opened, that these four contemplations are invited. You might like to connect to opening your body, heart, and mind as you engage with the next set of contemplations, while grounded in your anchor point, such as the breath.

DISCOURSE ON BREATHING MINDFULNESS:
Final Tetrad of Contemplations

13. Breathing in, I observe the impermanent nature of all phenomena. Breathing out, I observe the impermanent nature of all phenomena.

14. Breathing in, I observe the disappearance of desire. Breathing out, I observe the disappearance of desire.

15. Breathing in, I observe cessation. Breathing out, I observe cessation.

16. Breathing in, I observe letting go. Breathing out, I observe letting go.

Impermanence: Everything Changes

DISCOURSE ON BREATHING MINDFULNESS:
Thirteenth Contemplation

13. Breathing in, I observe the impermanent nature of all phenomena. Breathing out, I observe the impermanent nature of all phenomena.

Much of our lives are spent finding firm ground: finding a good-paying, stable career; finding a life partner; making enough money to enjoy pleasures in life and retire stably; buying a house; figuring out how to be happy and healthy. Most of us tell ourselves that everything will be fine after that, after that, after that. The challenge, and the opportunity, is that all phenomena, whether physiological, psychological, or physical, are changing—always. The millions-of-years-old Himalayan mountains are changing on a molecular basis as the weather slowly wears down the surfaces while tectonic plates thrust them upward on the southern front. Loved ones die; others break up with us. We get injured. Change can be hard.

Change can also be wonderful. Obesity is reversible. Final exam periods end. That phone call with a nagging parent comes to a conclusion. We can get physically stronger and wiser. Thank goodness. One of the beauties of neuroscience research is the discovery of neuroplasticity. Our brains can change throughout our lives. So can our bodies. We can grow, develop, and evolve. What changes can you harness?

When difficult change happens, can we suffer less as a result just by deeply knowing that change happens? Political regimes come and go. School programs come and go. Jobs come and go. The climate is changing. So are relationships. By knowing that, it can help us make sense of them when they do. We can also look for the opportunities within to harness, grow, and learn.

A lessen I learned from Joanne Friday is when challenging changes happen is to ask myself, "Do I want to be a victim or a student?" I prefer being a student so I learn, grow, and develop, and can then apply that wisdom to the next challenge. The trick is figuring out how to harness that change to take advantage of it. I invite you to, if you like, ask yourself: "What are you noticing changing in your life (for example, climate, digital technology, gig economy, high housing costs)?" Are there opportunities to harness the changes to take advantage of the opportunities there? For example, with regard to climate change, there are opportunities to develop technologies for storing sustainable solar and wind energy, conserve beautiful wild lands as carbon sinks, develop regenerative agriculture techniques, and leverage wisdom from indigenous peoples and others who deeply understand sustainability.

With the change toward increasingly high housing prices in certain areas, there are different ways we can respond, such as by moving to a beautiful emerging area in the country (or another country) that doesn't have high housing costs yet, matches who we are, and has opportunities in our areas of interest and expertise. Or another response to increasing housing prices, if it matches who we are, is to harness the energy from the stress of those high housing prices to foster career-related insights from what arises in the body, heart, mind, and spirit that will generate greater ethically sourced income for ourselves that we can then invest in real estate to allow us to live in that area. Many opportunities can arise once we accept that change happens and look for the opportunities within it.

A place where people can get caught in this teaching is feeling overwhelming anxiety that everything changes. Just because riding the wave of change can be empowering doesn't mean change itself can't feel destabilizing. If thinking about change makes you anxious, keep in mind that while everything changes, it also in many ways doesn't. There is stability too. Your emotionally closest family members will almost certainly always love you. While Mount Everest has shifted in terms of snowpack melt and the number of people climbing it, it is still a really big mountain that looms high on the roof of the world and will do so for millennia. *The magic is in holding both these truths—everything changes and there is stability—at the same time.* The destabilization that occurs while holding those two truths can allow us not to be attached to fixed ideas. The freedom within that then flows to allow us to be free of resistance to what is and can help us avoid having a meltdown when change happens. In fact, we can harness that freedom to keep ourselves innovative, personally growing, and placed at the forefront of our careers and society.

It is one thing to know on an intellectual level that everything changes, and it's another to have it fully accessible to you every moment of the day. Having the notion of impermanence hardwired so it is accessible moment by moment is what meditation can provide, especially when the object of meditation is impermanence itself. In fact, I would invite you to meditate on impermanence now, or if not right now, in the next day or so. So how about we try it out.

Impermanence Meditation

The intention of this meditation is, in an embodied nonintellectual way, to explore the fact that pretty much everything changes, practice accepting change, and then look at a particular emerging change in your life to see if there is an opportunity to take advantage of it in a way that would benefit you and world.

Taking a moment to set yourself up for a meditation, in a position that is comfortable and supports your alertness.

Connecting in with your anchor point of the breath, the body, or sound. Allowing your concentration to focus in on this object and only this object.

Recognizing thoughts as they arise, letting them pass by, and coming back to your anchor point.

Connecting with the body. Noticing what physical sensations are arising for you in this moment. Perhaps asking yourself, "Is the body open? If not, why not?" With an attitude of care, curiosity, nonjudgment, and understanding.

After some time, connecting with the emotions. Noticing what feeling tones are here, perhaps playing around with fostering joy and happiness.

Connecting in with the feeling tones and caring for them, even calming them.

If you like, asking, "Is my heart open? If not, why not?" And exploring the roots of any closures in your heart with kindness, particularly after you have had a little time to allow them to calm. Then considering what skillful next steps would allow the heart to open more, if it feels appropriate to do so. And taking those steps when the time is right.

Then as you like, connecting in with the mind, specifically the thoughts. Noticing what thoughts are bubbling up, perhaps racing along, or maybe meandering. Aware of the spaces between thoughts, if there are some.

Taking a moment, if you like, to gladden the mind, in an authentic way.

Now that you have worked with your mind a little, inviting you to concentrate the mind. Can you be right here, with this thought, this breath, this moment? If you like, using your anchor as an object to concentrate on.

And then, liberate the mind. Is anything causing it to constrict in this moment? In other words, asking yourself, "Is my mind open? If not, why not?" And can you invite the mind to let go of any hindrances that are causing it to constrict and be here in this moment, being just who you are?

As you are ready, and if you are ready, inviting you to consider, while connected to your anchor point: I observe the impermanent nature of all phenomena. In other words, everything changes.

Just noticing your physical sensations, emotions, and thoughts as you offer yourself this contemplation, and returning to your anchor point of the breath, body, or sound to stay grounded when helpful.

Exploring whether you can think of anything that doesn't change.

If you think there is something that doesn't change, perhaps ask yourself, "Am I sure?"

If the answer is yes, then, as my mindfulness teacher Joanne Friday would encourage, ask again.

Perhaps exploring if we can not only intellectually, but in an embodied, hardwired way, accept that change happens and is even inevitable.

In doing so, can we harness and take advantage of the opportunities within?

Or at least perhaps not have a fit when change does happen?

Exploring now if there is a change that is currently happening in yourself, your life, or even your surroundings, such as the environment, the economy, your career field, or in someone you care for. Consider this change, perhaps asking yourself, "Is there is an opportunity to harness that change in a way that would be of benefit to me and world?"

What might it be?

How can you take advantage of that change and ride that opportunity like a wave?

As this contemplation comes to a close, inviting you to return to your anchor point, settling in, and inviting the awareness or insights that came from this meditation, if any did, to transition into the next part of your day.

I'm glad that we are now completely comfortable with impermanence and got that out of the way. Now it's just a simple matter of letting go of desire and craving for experiences and material items that don't actually bring happiness. Shall we explore this opportunity to build character together? You might like to take a little break first.

The Disappearance of Desire

DISCOURSE ON BREATHING MINDFULNESS:
Fourteenth Contemplation

14. *Breathing in, I observe the disappearance of desire. Breathing out, I observe the disappearance of desire.*

Another translation of this contemplation is "Contemplating dispassion, I breathe in. Contemplating dispassion, I breathe out" (Shaw 2006).

In this section, we will explore our relationship with some potential traps, you know, like sex, money, power, tasty food, and sleep. Some of us have unhealthy desires or cravings toward them; others of us have unhealthy aversions toward them. The exploration here is how to let go of unhealthily desiring them or unhealthily avoiding them and find a balance that is healthy for you and those who you influence. "Disappearance of desire" in this context is the absence of longing for something in a striving or clenching kind of way.

Another place where desirelessness is fruitful is in relation to the eight vicissitudes, also called the "eight worldly winds," which are four sets of opposing experiences. They are pleasure and pain, gain and loss, praise and blame, and fame and disrepute. We often have unhealthy cravings for pleasure, gain, praise, and fame, and unhealthy aversions to pain, loss, blame, and disrepute. The truth, my friend, and if you can get comfortable with this, is that life has all eight. There really isn't anything we can do about it.

You may well be judging what you are reading right now (blame), or maybe you think it is awesome (praise). I really can't do much about it. People will praise us and blame us. Gain will come (such as a job promotion, getting into a great college, having a baby) as will loss (say, of a romantic partner, an athletic competition, a close grandparent). The trick is not to take any of the eight worldly winds all that seriously because they all come and go, just like the wind outside our home. In doing so, we are just ourselves, and we become fearless. Life gets easier to navigate. And, a funny side effect when we let go of craving and aversion to these factors is the more positive experiences often start showing up more.

Dana, a student who went through MBC and developed a strong mindfulness meditation practice, shared one of the moments when she realized it worked. At the time she had been dating a guy for almost a year, and they were pretty serious. Everything was going fine, as far as Dana was concerned. They hadn't been fighting. She went away for a five-day meditation retreat. When she came back, he broke up with her.

Dana was just getting ready for her first medical school interview in two days. The timing was terrible, and she had a right to be upset by the feelings of loss and pain, two of the vicissitudes described above. And she did feel sad. She just wasn't so upset. Luckily, she was feeling grounded from the retreat and able not get caught in craving for the relationship to be something other than it was. Instead, she was able to accept what was happening and focus on preparing for her interview. In time, she shifted the relationship to a friendship and grew in areas of her life, including other relationships that bring her joy and fulfillment. She got into one of the top medical schools in the United States, as we will see shortly.

So how can we work with desireless, or letting go of craving, in a healthy way? Below is an opportunity to give it a shot.

Desirelessness Meditation

The intention of this meditation is to free ourselves from unhelpful desires and cravings for things that don't actually bring net happiness to ourselves or others, while still being able to make plans. Nonstriving (not grasping for outcomes in ways that bring us out of the present moment) is an element that we are encouraged foster in mindfulness practice, but we also need to plan for the future. This meditation is designed to help you simultaneously hold both elements, in other words hold both desirelessness (or nonstriving) and setting an intention for what you what to bring into your life more in the future. In doing so, I hope it will support you in making plans that will help you succeed, boost well-being, and build the life you want in ways that match who you truly are.

> Similar to the last contemplation, taking a moment to check in with yourself, grounding yourself first in your anchor point, and then in time, seeing if you can allow your body, mind, and heart to open.
>
> Settling in and seeing what is arising for you in terms of what you would deeply like as a skillful next step for yourself.
>
> Is it a trip somewhere?
>
> Is it letting go eating of a certain food?
>
> Is it setting a time limit on your social media use?
>
> Maybe asking that person you are romantically interested in to go for a walk or hang out in another way that might be a good fit for both of you?
>
> What is it in terms of you true self that is aligned with your values that you would like to express out?
>
> Following is a set of questions that is grounded in motivational interviewing. As you consider the questions, can you do so in a way that is letting go of craving and aversion? By this, I really mean letting go of

the clenching, or the grasping, of your goal. Instead, can it just be a natural part of you expressing out?

What is an intention that you would like to set for the coming week?

1. *On a scale of 1–10, where 10 is high, how motivated are you to achieve this intention?*

2. *On a scale of 1–10, how confident are you that you will achieve the intention?*

3. *What could you do that would raise your motivation or confidence a little?*

4. *What might make it difficult to achieve the intention this week, and if that happens, what will you do?*

5. *How could you measure this intention in a way that resonates with you?*

In time, you would be welcome to share this intention with someone, such as a parent or friend, as having that social support sometimes helps to act on the goal.

Here in many ways, we are holding both desirelessness and desire at the same time, and in doing so, releasing ourselves from the craving or aversion—the grasping and clenching that can get in the way of us just being who we are and of our naturally expressed power and creativity because we are focused on some outcome at the expense of something maybe even more important that has arisen in this moment.

Inviting you to set an intention for the week but one that is as free as possible of craving and aversion.

Setting an intention or a goal can lead to some longing to be something or someone other than who we are. It can create feelings of striving, which can take us out of the present moment. When setting an intention, I encourage you to hold both setting an intention and avoiding unwholesome desire for it (striving or craving) at the same time. Opening ourselves to our body, heart, mind, and spirit can allow us to see our true selves within.

That is how to set an intention: by setting an intention that brings us closer to who we already are—who we truly are that is consistent with our values, mind, and body. Maybe your true self is more physically fit or socially connected. Maybe your true self is less distracted by social media and more connected to your friends and family. As you consider your intentions for the coming week in this chapter, I invite you to work with the concept of desirelessness: just be who you are, letting go of attachment to sex, sleep, tasty food, money, power, fame, gain, pleasure, and praise, while letting go of any aversion to those factors as well as others, such as loss, blame, pain, and disrepute. By letting go of those unwholesome desires, we can bloom into the flower that we are naturally meant to be, thereby serving ourselves and those around us. If that is done well, it may lead to great power, fame, money, praise, gain, and pleasure...but that's not the point.

Cessation

Discourse on Breathing Mindfulness: Fifteenth Contemplation

15. Breathing in, I observe cessation. Breathing out, I observe cessation.

Anther translation of this contemplation is "Breathing in, I observe the no-birth, no-death nature of all phenomena. Breathing out, I observe the no-birth, no-death nature of all phenomena" (Nhat Hanh 2007).

The Pāli word *nirodha* is often translated as "cessation," which refers to quenching or extinction. It refers to the cessation of ignorance—where we see nature (basically everything) for what it really is. Doing so can free us from individuality so we see how we are simply a part of the universe. It can help us connect with the ultimate reality. We can let go of some of our biggest fears, such as fear of birth, aging, illness, and death. In this section I will focus first on freeing ourselves from fear of death.

Fear of death is a big one for many of us. However, in many ways, we are born and die every day. Estimates show that as many as one hundred trillion cells in the body die every day, and the same number are born (Gilbert 2000). That translates to more than a million cells being born and dying in us *every second*. At a cellular level, we are different every moment of the day. Physiologically, you are a different person now than when you first started reading this sentence. Carbon, oxygen, nitrogen, and many other elements and molecules flow in and out of living and nonliving beings on a molecular level, spreading across the world and indeed the universe. In fact, estimates suggest that we have had molecules in our bodies that were also in the bodies of pretty much everyone in the world, such as Jesus, Mohammad, and the Beatles. Life is amazing.

This morning, I picked a bouquet of flowers for Betsy to celebrate our wedding anniversary and placed them in a vase on the breakfast table. It brought a smile to her and my daughters' faces as they sat down. In a week, they will be in our compost bin, decomposing with the fruit, vegetables, and leaves. Next spring or fall, I will spread the compost on the garden, and the molecules in it will become that year's flowers. The cycle of life begs the questions: When was the flower born, and when did it die? Or is it just a cycle of molecules moving through different phases of reality?

When those we love die, they often find their way into our lives in different manifestations. For example, Serena, who recently graduated from my Meditation, Mindfulness, and Health course, shared that her grandfather passed away during the course. It was her first close family member that had passed on. She traveled to Oklahoma for his service. During that time, she noticed how a lot of what her mom and her siblings said included the "no birth, no death" teaching. She explained, "There's no way I can think he is completely gone because he is still here in all of his daughters and grandchildren. Nobody really dies because parts of them are in us." During the service, Serena's mom described characteristics of her father present in each of his grandchildren. Serena shared, "In my brother is my grandfather's quiet curiosity—they are both shy, smart, curious people. In me is my grandfather's love of music. In my cousin, his caring, giving personality. Every part of his personality shows up in each of us." This teaching of no birth and no death shows that each of us infuses others with who we are, with our teachings and realizations, and even with the molecules we breathe. In fact, Serena's grandfather's qualities are infused in this book, and now you. When are birth and death really, and do they even exist?

Returning to the flowers in the compost, when they have turned into rich compost, I will spread the compost over our vegetable garden. There the molecules from the flowers, including the carbon and nitrogen, will infuse into the soil and be drawn into the roots of the kale we grow. When we harvest that kale and blend it into one of our morning smoothies, we will find ourselves happily consuming elements of those flowers through our stomach, instead of through our eyes as we did the year before. Is this the new birth of the flowers in their next form? Is their new form us?

Coming back to Dana, now at Duke University in her first year of medical school, she feels grateful to be doing human anatomy dissections. She explained that it teaches her much about the body but can at times be disturbing and emotionally intense. On her first day in the anatomy room, Dana took a few moments to be with the donor who offered his body for dissection. The donor could have elected to be buried or cremated, but he donated his body to science so students like Dana could better help the living. She was grateful for his life and what it allowed the students to learn.

In considering the concept of no birth, and no death, Dana shared, "It very much feels like a continuation of this person's life. It's like he is coming alive every day in some ways because he is teaching us." In many ways birth and death is just a cycle of molecules, knowledge, and wisdom moving places. When we look closely, it is not easy, and perhaps impossible, to pinpoint an exact moment of birth and death. It is just a continuation. Because of this, Thich Nhat Hanh refers to his birthday as his "continuation day."

While we can get all soft and squishy about there being no birth and no death, at the same time, there is birth and death. Babies come out of their mothers' wombs on a certain day and at a certain time. In fact, our mothers probably know the exact day and time we arrived. Our loved ones who passed away took their last breath at a particular moment. Can we hold both the concept of birth and death and the concept of no birth and no death simultaneously? They are both true. And in holding them at the same time, it can destabilize us in potentially helpful ways that free us from rigid forms of thinking about some of the greatest causes of fear in many people's lives—such as death. Fear can cause the spirit to close, but working with this contemplation and the insights that arise can allow fear to disappear, wisdom to arise, and the spirit to open. You can become fearless.

In some ways, if you believe this line of reasoning, isn't it lovely to know that we and our loved ones never really die? We just change form. While the concept of no birth and no death can be freeing, it can also be a place where some of us get caught in incomplete understanding.

There's a story about a Buddhist teacher who said that one of his biggest regrets was advising an older man not to train in an advanced Buddhist teaching given his age. The teacher felt it was better to only take on that training when we are younger and have time to really work through it. Sadly, the older man, who believed in rebirth and wanted to come back younger and able to work on that advanced teaching, died by suicide. The teacher used his energy of regret over that incident to deepen his practice and to serve others as skillfully as he could from that point forward. Destabilizing our ideas around birth and death is not an invitation to deemphasize the value of our lives now. In fact, it is designed to release us from rigid thinking and the fear of death so we can enjoy this moment and this life even more.

If you like, taking a moment to reflect on birth and death.

No-Birth, No-Death Meditation

The intention of this meditation is to explore the continuity of all beings independent of their "birth" and "death." In doing so, it may free you from unhelpful fears of death, thereby enabling you live even more fully now.

Perhaps considering someone who had a positive influence on you who is no longer alive. It could be a grandparent or a wise figure, such as Gandhi, Martin Luther King Jr., or Mother Teresa.

If you are struggling to find someone who is no longer alive, it's okay to pick someone who is alive.

Taking a moment to reflect on this person, bringing them visually to mind.

Now, calling up something specific that they taught you, that you carry in you now. It may be a lesson, a way of being, or an insightful or funny story.

Considering, if you like, the idea that when we die, all that we leave behind are the results of our actions. What results of actions did they leave behind?

Considering how in some ways, through their actions, including the positive ones you were reflecting on, that elements of who they were now live inside you. That you and others whose lives they touched are a continuation of them.

Inviting you to consider the millions of years that the world has existed and perhaps considering how our lives are just a brief moment in time.

We are a just continuation of our ancestors and others who influenced us and are the results of animals, plants, and minerals that have also enabled us to be who we currently are.

How best do you want to live this life, and what do you want to leave behind as your continuation?

Emptiness of a Separate Self: Interbeing

Betsy and I recently bought a beautiful, handcrafted bureau. This bureau wouldn't have manifested if the two of us had not selected the type of wood, size, and the finish. It would not have been made without the skilled carpenters who dedicated their time and training to crafting it. Furthermore, if it weren't for the birch trees that grew the wood, this particular bureau would not have occurred. If it weren't for the logger who cut the birches down, this specific bureau with this wood never would have arrived in our home. If it weren't for the sun and the rain, the birches never would have grown. Each molecule of carbon dioxide that the trees breathed in and became part of the wood came from around the world over millennia, inhabiting different beings at different times. In fact, in many ways, the entire cosmos is in that bureau. That bureau *inter-is* with just about everything. Everything is connected. How cool is that? It's one thing to understand interconnectedness, or interbeing, at the conceptual level and another to have it as a tool that is available to us every moment of the day.

The concept of interbeing, or emptiness of a separate self, can be very freeing. It can free us from our ego and narcissistic tendencies, for example. Take our personality. It is what it is. In fact, more specifically, our personality is a combination of our environment and biology. The environment includes our family, friends, social media, culture, country, language, and many other factors. Biology includes genetics. We are increasingly realizing it also involves epigenetics, or the protein structure around DNA that turns genes on and off. It also likely includes the microbiome, which is the colony of microbes that live in and on us, equaling about the number of cells as our own body. Each of those influences our personality. Those genes come from a long line of ancestors. If your great-great-great-great-great-grandmother had not passed on her DNA, you wouldn't be here.

Who we are is just a transition between our teachers, family, influences, biology, food, environment, and many other things and the next generation of what we become. Who are we but a continuation of passing along what we were given by others? Not a single idea in this book is mine. As you can see from all my teachers' and the young adults' stories, I am passing on their wisdom. We are just conduits from the past to the future. Are we really all that? Yep. And nope. Who are "we" other than the entire interconnected planet and arguably the universe?

There are benefits to contemplating this teaching of interbeing, or emptiness of separate self. First, letting go of thinking of ourselves as a separate self relieves us of pride and narcissism that our accomplishments are because of us. Second, it gives us a break if we blame ourselves for not being more than we could be. Maybe we have a learning disability. Maybe a physical disability. Maybe post-traumatic stress disorder. Maybe we didn't get into our top college choice or missed out on our dream job. There are many causes and conditions that went into any one of those things. Some may be genetic. Some are environmental. We are only in part responsible for who we are. Knowing that can provide compassion and understanding toward ourselves that is not just kind self-talk, but reality. Third, it can help us consider how interdependent we are on each other and the environment. The microplastics used in shampoo make their way into the sewer system, out into the oceans and rivers, into the fish, and back into our bodies. That pesticide-covered orange peel that I considered putting into my compost would go into my vegetable garden and becomes next year's carrot that my daughter eats. This understanding of our interconnectedness can provide not only wisdom, but also the energy to care for each of us more, whether it is people, animals, plants, or minerals.

Where people get caught in this teaching—which is one that can cause difficulties—is the idea of "no self": that our self doesn't exit. It does. When Thich Nhat Hanh (1998) teaches the principal of "no self," he instead emphasizes "emptiness of a separate self" and "interbeing." I find that approach not only clearer but also reduces the risk for confusion.

As in the teachings above on "no birth, no death" and on "everything changes," we are empty of a separate self. And, importantly, we have a separate self. There is a bag of skin surrounding us and a body and mind inside. Both realities exist, and these are just words attempting to bring us to a deeper understanding of reality. Can we hold both realities simultaneously and not grasp either too tightly? In that in-between space, the true self in all its richness may appear more strongly.

Zen master Qingyuan Weixin famously wrote: "Before I had studied Zen for thirty years, I saw mountains as mountains, and waters as waters. When I arrived at a more intimate knowledge, I came to the point where I saw that mountains are not mountains, and waters are not waters. But now that I have got its very substance I am at rest. For it's just that I see mountains once again as mountains, and waters once again as waters" (Watts 1951). With these teachings, it is like we are unpacking birth, death, change, and self. We see their individual components, and then we still need to call them something. We can call them birth, death, change, and self but perhaps not take them so seriously, have greater wisdom about them, and in the process open ourselves to simply what is. By realizing that, it can open our spirit to be who we naturally are and how the world around us works.

These are just some examples of domains that may serve to open the spirit. Or may not. In my opinion, you hold the greatest wisdom for what that is in you. I encourage you to reflect on what practices in your life create openings. Mahatma Gandhi, in his autobiography *The Story of My Experiments with Truth*, shared how he ran his life like a series of experiments. He kept doing what worked and letting go of doing what didn't. I invite you to run a series of experiments testing which practices or actions in your life create awakenings for you. Maybe it is doing one or more of the contemplations above on a regular basis. Maybe it is connecting with a particular prayer or a self-care practice. As you find what the effective practices are, I invite you to bring them into your life, while letting go of anything that is ineffective.

Letting Go

DISCOURSE ON BREATHING MINDFULNESS:
Final Contemplation

16. Breathing in, I observe letting go. Breathing out, I observe letting go.

With this contemplation, we are letting go of anything that is causing us to suffer unnecessarily. It could, for example, be letting go of a behavior (such as smoking or yelling at a loved one), a way of thinking (such as racial bias or being judgmental), a material item (such as that huge ugly dresser that your relative gave you), a romantic partner who is not a good match, or a career path. Letting go can be challenging, but with the power of mindfulness training in self-awareness, attention control, and emotion regulation, it happens. Neuroplasticity helps us let go of self-limiting habits and replace them with new behaviors that can help us succeed, boost our well-being, and build the life we want.

If you've ever seen a cattle field, you've probably noticed foot paths from their repetitive travel habits. The neural networks in our brains are like cow paths. We naturally create thinking "paths" that become second nature. Sometimes, these thinking habits were formed when we were children, before our brains were fully developed. Those thinking patterns result in actions. For example, we may have witnessed our father disparaging his sister when she was not around, so we started to make fun of our sibling when she was not around. It may not be the most skillful approach, but it became a habit before our brains were fully developed without us even really knowing it.

The wonderful thing about mindfulness is that it fosters self-awareness (maybe we start to notice, *I am putting down my sibling again.... Why do I do that?*) and attention control (*Can I spend some time meditating and looking deeply into why I disparage my sister?*), which can cycle between the two (*Huh, I saw my dad do that to his sibling. But now that I am an adult, I see there is a better way*) and start to unwind that habit and form a new one (*I am going to feel compassion for my sister. In fact, next time I see her, I'm going to let her know that I am here for her*).

This creates new neural networks in the brain, and we can let go of the old neural networks, or habits or thought patterns and paths, that no longer serve us, just like cattle create new paths when they find fresh grass and a new water source. We may still find ourselves in an old thought pattern at some point—the old paths are still there, but they fill in over time when the paths are used less often, and then we can use our mindfulness powers of self-awareness and attention control to move to a new path.

In fact, one of the most compelling scientific discoveries in brain physiology is that mindfulness meditation seems to not only alter specific regions of the brain, but it enhances the connectivity between regions of the brain (Gotink et al. 2016). There is functional magnetic resonance imaging (fMRI) evidence showing that new functional paths form in our brains as a result of mindfulness meditation practice, which fosters wiser decision making and involves various regions of the brain, ultimately leading to greater wisdom.

Twyla, a varsity diver at Brown, shared how she used mindfulness and the concept of letting go during competitions. "Mindfulness helped me work with emotional and physical pain because I had a lot of fear when I dove, and it helped me get over that." During a competition when she was midair performing a diving routine, she hit her hands on the diving board. Reflecting on that event, she shared, "I was able to think, *Okay, let's take a moment to witness pain and what is going on*. I would witness the physical pain first. And that helped with the emotional pain. So much of my fear of pain or my reaction to pain in diving and in general was rooted in that I never just took time to feel it. It was always a reaction to the pain. By being able to sit with the physical pain and witness it, the reaction sort of melted away. It allowed me to both come toward the emotional and physical pain and care for it, and then in doing so, it allowed me to let go of the rumination on it and prepare to be 100 percent present for the next dive."

Are there particular habits or thoughts you have that you would like to let go of? Below is a meditation on that.

Letting Go Meditation

The intention of this meditation is to connect with the mind and body and explore if we have any behaviors or patterns that are self-limiting. Through a better understanding of what we get from the self-limiting pattern, both benefits and harms, we can then make a more considered decision on letting that pattern or behavior go if it has a net negative effect. Perhaps, through our improving attention control, self-awareness, and emotion regulation, we can replace a self-limiting behavior or pattern with a new one that provides a net benefit to us and others.

Taking a moment to settle in for a meditation, inviting the eyes to close most of the way while you find your way to your anchor point of the breath, body, or sound.

Recognizing thoughts, emotions, and physical sensations as they arise. Noting them, and then returning to your anchor point, giving your body and mind a chance to focus and get centered.

Taking a moment to check in with the thoughts and emotions. What's here?

Are the heart and mind open?

Are they clenched or agitated in any way? If so, connecting in with that. Witnessing the element that is causing your heart or mind to be closed, constrained, or agitated.

Encouraging you to stay in your comfort or growth zone, and if you reach an overwhelmed zone, you can always pause on this exercise or connect in with your anchor point or another healthy distraction.

Caring for the element that is causing agitation in the emotions and thoughts.

Once it has calmed a little, as often happens when we take the time to turn toward it with kindness and curiosity and without judgment, seeing what roots are there.

Perhaps asking yourself: "How do I or others benefit from this thought pattern or behavior?"

It's likely that you benefit in some way, either now or did in the past. Why else would you do it?

Also, if you like, ask: "How is this thought pattern or behavior a disservice to me and others? What is the net benefit?"

Just being honest with yourself, whatever the answers are, whether there is a net benefit or net disservice.

Then, through being with that habit or thought pattern deeply, while respecting your limits, if you would like to, let it go, and replace it with a pattern that serves you and others better.

Returning to your anchor point of the breath, body, or sound as this meditation comes to a close.

Using our meditation-trained skill of self-awareness, we can identify the thoughts or behaviors that are limiting us from being our true selves. We can even identify what our true self is. Then, with our training in attention control, we can better let debilitating patterns go and replace them with thoughts or behaviors that will lead to what Jud Brewer called a "bigger, better offer" in his book *Unwinding Anxiety*, as we are likely to do things that provide us with rewards. For me, often my bigger, better offer is greater happiness and well-being and seeing that I am causing less harm to my family, friends, and coworkers as a result of letting a thought or behavior go and replacing it with a more skillful one. What is it for you?

Many Contemplative Traditions Open the Spirit

There are many ways to open the spirit, and it seems most of the respected wisdom traditions that have stood the test of time developed technologies to do so. Opening to the spirit or connecting to a higher power can help us get out of our own way. If you practice in a wisdom tradition, such as Christianity, Islam, Judaism, Sufiism, Hinduism, Buddhism, Native American spirituality, or really any wisdom tradition, I invite you to use it to open your spirit. Think of the bumper sticker that says, "What would Jesus do?" There is a decent amount of wisdom to that simple question (fill in the blank instead of "Jesus" if you are of a different spiritual tradition and have a different higher power or sources of wisdom that you connect to), as it helps us get out of ourselves, take a step back, and ask what a wise one would feel is the most skillful next step in the situation. In many ways, there is one "room" (for example, an open spirit), but many doors to that room. What doors best suit you? I encourage you to respect your spiritual roots and dovetail any learnings in this chapter with practices you know take you there.

Opening the Spirit Meditation

The intention of this meditation is to first ground yourself in your body, heart, and mind, and then explore opening the spirit so your full wisdom can be woven into your moment-to-moment life, allowing you to be fully expressed and wise in every action that you take.

> Taking a moment, and checking in with your anchor point, maybe it is the breath, the body, or sound.
>
> Inviting you to check in with your body, opening it, or seeing what is causing it to be closed.
>
> Then, in time, inviting you to open your heart, even asking if it is open and if not, why not.

Then moving to the mind, seeing if it is open or what is causing it to close if it is closed.

Seeing if you can work with those roots of the closures to loosen the knot of whatever is bound up causing the mind not to be open.

Seeing if you can loosen any knots, even just a little bit, to bring more opening in the body, heart, and mind.

And now shifting to check in with your spirit. Is it feeling open? If not, why not?

Being gentle here, offering kindness and compassion to whatever may be causing the spirit to be closed. Understanding the roots of that closure in time and seeing what arises around skillful next steps that would help heal those roots and allow your spirit to open more. Perhaps considering approaches you've learned in this book such as in the Discourse on Breathing Mindfulness or in another wisdom tradition to allow your spirit to open more.

What is here?

What is being communicated to you, and is there wisdom in it?

Does it resonate with who you are?

Maybe write it down, jotting it on your smartphone or in a journal.

As this contemplation comes to a close, returning your concentration to your anchor point of the breath, body, or sound, settling in there as long as you like before shifting on to the next part of your day, perhaps bringing any learnings from this contemplation into it.

There is great wisdom in our hearts, minds, bodies, and spirits. By opening to them, even for brief moments, we can allow that wisdom to manifest, and thereby benefit not only ourselves, but the world around us. In the next chapter, we will explore practical ways to apply these openings to ourselves, such as our careers, performance, and more.

Home Practices

1. What is it in this chapter, or in a wisdom tradition that resonates with you, that opens your spirit? I invite you to work with that most days this week.

2. Several times this week, work with the last tetrad of contemplations in the Discourse on Breathing Mindfulness offered in this chapter. In each session, I'd recommend first warming up by doing a meditation that grounds yourself in your anchor point (breath, body, or sound) and then working on connecting with your physical sensations (first tetrad of contemplations in the discourse), emotions (second tetrad), and mind (third tetrad). Then as you have this base, begin to consider the new contemplations (fourth tetrad), such as impermanence. Appendix 2 lists all sixteen contemplations so you can see them in one place.

3. Many times this week, I invite you to work with the meditation on opening the body, heart, mind, and spirit. Grounding first in your anchor point of the breath, body, or sound, and then asking yourself, "Is my body open? If not, why not?" Continue in sequence with similar self-reflection questions on opening the heart, mind, and spirit, knowing you can always come back to your anchor point to get grounded. What do the contemplations bring up for you? Can you act on what arises in skillful ways?

CHAPTER 5

Practical Applications for Ourselves

Career, Performance, Social Media Use, and More

This chapter dives into how to apply the openings in the heart, body, mind, and spirit to this moment, right now. To this life. Wherever you are. That is where the rubber meets the road. This chapter is about applying mindfulness to your daily life.

Deep in the brain is a nerve pathway called the default mode network. It connects the medial prefrontal cortex to the anterior cingulate cortex, and it's responsible for that feeling when you are on "default." It could be daydreaming about a trip you've been on or ruminating about why someone said that nasty thing. The term for this state is "self-referential processing," which is thinking about things in relation to ourselves. One of the most consistently replicated findings in mindfulness neuroscience is that meditation appears to quiet this pathway (Brewer et al. 2011). It lets us be here and now, rather than wandering to the future or the past, thinking about how things relate to us.

I mentioned in the last chapter that meditation also seems to promote formation of neural networks between different areas of the brain. That is one of the most important discoveries because it suggests meditation allows us to use more of our entire brain in collaboration with itself. Instead of one region dominating (such as the fight-or-flight center in the amygdala), they talk to each other, which leads to better decisions. The different regions of our brain are incredibly powerful, and each plays a different role. When they all work in harmony with each other, it can unleash abilities we never knew were possible.

Think of someone you know or have seen who is physically chiseled. Did that musculature happen by chance? Of course not. They worked hard at it, and the muscles appeared as result. Perhaps think of someone you know who is wise. Did that happen randomly? No. They worked at it too. Think of Mahatma Gandhi, who fasted for weeks to foster nonviolence and societal equality; the Dalai Lama, who escaped in disguise by horseback over the Himalayas into northern India at the age of twenty-three and witnessed his friends and fellow Tibetans killed while being a political and spiritual leader; Mother Teresa, who dedicated her life to work with the lowest of the low castes while being discriminated against as a woman; and Martin Luther King Jr., who faced racial persecution and gave voice to others with kindness and a strong sense of community. These people turned toward some of the greatest suffering of our time, learned from it, and applied it to other areas of life. As a result, they are recognized worldwide for their wisdom, all have been nominated for the Nobel Peace Prize, and three have won it. What they modeled and taught others grew from deep experience and wisdom.

Just like wisdom and working out, changing the brain doesn't happen overnight. We have to practice mindfulness pretty much every day, preferably in community with a skilled teacher, if we want big results. Then the mind and body build those networks that allow regions in the brain to change, such as the default mode network to quiet, the hippocampus to strengthen the memory, and the prefrontal cortex to better connect with the amygdala, so when a stressor arrives, fast action with logic and reason come through in response. Evidence supports this.

A systematic review of forty-three mindfulness intervention studies showed that participants who practiced more had stronger outcomes (Parsons et al. 2017). However, at the same time, it may be a little like riding a bike, where once you know it, you've got it forever. For example, in our Mindfulness-Based Blood Pressure (MB-BP) Reduction clinical trial, the frequency that participants practiced meditation during the course predicted their blood pressure one year later, regardless of how much time they practiced after the course was over (Loucks et al. 2019). In fact, the practice that took place during the course itself was a better predictor of blood pressure a year later, compared to doing the mindfulness practices after the course was completed. Health outcomes are likely a combination of the quality and quantity of practice, and any amount may well serve for the long term due to the insights that arise and change us.

This means the hard work we put into opening the body, heart, mind, and spirit, even if it is just in a quiet room sitting on a cushion, is very likely to translate into the rest of the day. Practice prepares the neural networks. Just like someone who works out regularly has the muscles available to help you move your couch, the time we spend in meditation develops our strength in areas such as self-awareness, attention control, loving-kindness, and emotion regulation so those skills are there when we need them. Below, I introduce some examples of applications of mindfulness practice. Books could be written about mindfulness applications for each of these, and likely have, so my goal is to just plant some seeds that may germinate in time.

Using Mindfulness to Clarify the Best Career Path

When I taught the senior seminar course to Brown School of Public Health undergraduate students, which was designed to be a culminating experience for their college degree, one of the first slides I showed was figure 5.1. I would give students time to reflect on these questions:

What is important for the world?

What are your natural and learned skills?

What do you naturally like to think about?

What are doable jobs in the field?

I would then invite them to look for the sweet spot career-wise that shares a similar answer for all four questions. Part of their coursework was to interview two people who had positions in that sweet spot to get a real-life feel for the work involved. There is a guided meditation on this later in the chapter.

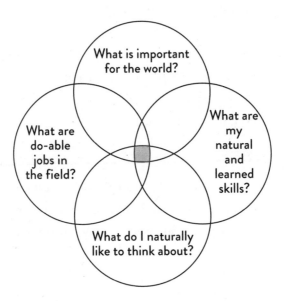

Figure 5.1   Four questions for self-reflection to identify a successful career path. Identify answers in the sweet spot where all four circles overlap.

People who have been both happy and successful in their career often broke free from societal expectations of them, parental expectations, and honestly, their own poorly informed expectations of themselves. They often came to know themselves better, came to know the world better, and found a match between who they naturally were and what they wanted to do for their career.

My Ngoc was about halfway through a ten-day meditation retreat and was experiencing lot of leg pain from sitting cross-legged. She had recently applied to medical school for the second time, and it wasn't going the way she hoped. Also, she wasn't sure medicine was what she wanted to do with her life, despite it being a socially respected career. She was watching the leg pain and with surprise, noticed the pain disappear. She realized in that moment a sense of lack of an independent self (covered in chapter 4) and that she didn't need to hold on to the pain. In fact, in that moment, she realized that she was holding a lot of ideas of who she was and who she "needed" to be (such as a medical doctor), and a lot of insights arose out of that emotional and physical pain about what she could let go of and who she really was.

After the meditation, she shared, "It occurred to me that the experience translated onto the bigger picture of who I am. Who I thought I was isn't who I am. I am more than that. From that deeper space, I was able to access the deeper truth about who I really am and what I really care about: helping, relationships, and people. That led me into social work that I have been very, very happy with. I realized I didn't want to be in the biomedical model of operating. I care a lot about advocacy, social justice, and directly serving traumatized and marginalized populations, and I wanted to be seated in a field that puts that at its forefront."

Thich Nhat Hanh (1991) teaches a practice for processing a strong emotion. He suggests caring for it like a parent would a crying child. Then, after the emotion is cared for in a compassionate, kind, gentle way, see if it's possible to look deeply into the roots of that emotion. Once we understand the roots, such as My Ngoc did, a clearer path can open up, and that could be a career path or a path for improving our work performance.

Below is a meditation focused on your career path that you might like to try.

Career Path Meditation

The intention of this meditation is to first connect with your body, heart, mind, and spirit and then answer a series of questions to identify your career sweet spot. The sweet spot addresses not only what is important for the world, but also the area you like to naturally think about, that uses your natural and learned skills, and that has doable jobs in the field. This is the place where you can be well expressed, doing work that you are good at, enjoy, and the world needs.

Inviting you to get out something that you can write or type on, like a journal, scrap of paper, laptop, or smartphone. Putting that item down beside you and getting ready for a contemplation. Closing the eyes most of the way, if you are comfortable with that, except, of course, when you are reading the contemplations below.

Finding your way to your anchor of the breath, a part of the body (palms of the hands, soles of the feet), or sound. Spending some time with focused attention on that anchor point, noticing when the mind wanders, and with gentleness, bringing it back to that anchor point.

Bringing awareness to physical sensations. Is the body open in this moment? If not, why not?

Checking in with the heart, with the emotions. Is the heart open? If not, why not?

How about the mind? Is it open? And the spirit? Tending to them if they are closed and inviting them to open if they are ready.

Connect in with figure 5.1. Inviting you to reflect on the questions:

What is important for the world at this time in history? What is needed?

Even listing your responses on what you have beside you to write on.

As you are ready, inviting you to reflect, with an open body, heart, mind, and spirit:

What are my natural and learned skills?

Even writing these strength areas down, if you like.

Next, asking yourself: "What do I naturally like to think about?

When I am wandering down the road, or taking a shower, where does my mind go?"

If you can find a career path that taps into what you naturally like to think about, then suddenly your down time is productive for work.

Now shifting over to the self-reflection: What are doable jobs in the field?

These might be ones that have a good number of job openings right now, for example, or that at least a have decent salary. This is a reality-check question to make sure the career path you hope for is likely attainable for you.

Now, inviting you to look for the sweet spot where the circles in figure 5.1 overlap. What is important for the world AND you like to naturally think about AND utilizes your natural and learned skills AND has doable jobs in the field? Is anything arising for you in these areas? Are there any questions you might like to answer through your own research and talking with people in that field?

As you are ready, returning to your anchor point of the breath, body, or sound, taking a moment to get grounded before continuing on with your next steps of the day.

Using Mindfulness to Improve Work Performance

Camille, a research consultant, shared, "Mindfulness principles are so helpful in keeping me in this moment. In the past, I could spin out on all the things I had to do. That could stop me from doing them. Now I have a better realization that there is nothing I have to do other than what I am doing now. That has been so helpful managing my professional life. For example, I do a lot of writing. When you haven't written anything and then have to write something, getting started can be so challenging. Mindfulness helps me chunk it into 'this one word' and 'this one sentence' in this moment. It has transformed my ability to write. I have become faster and more expressive. I like to write, but it's been anxiety provoking, and now it's much less so."

Camille also found that mindfulness practice helped her time management. "It has helped me be more intentional in carving out time to land in my body and my experience, to check in with myself. I have been trying to have at least three check-in points in the day: when I wake up, before or after lunch, and before I go to bed. I might take a short walk, do a short guided session, or do a little yoga. Having these small touch points during the day has helped me be more productive, focus my priorities, and bring me into a rhythm where I slow down and check in. It's not straight up time management, but it's helping me find pockets of time to take care of myself, which has then helped other areas of my life as well. Mindfulness is great about preventing procrastination and helping me just start the work. Once you have gotten started, it is never as daunting as it seems before you start."

Many people have expressed how mindfulness helps reduce procrastination and increase focus on the most important work (and life) priorities. For example, once I shared with my mindfulness teacher Joanne Friday that I was stressed about all the work tasks I was facing, and I asked her how she manages this kind of thing. She shared that she prioritizes what is the most important task and does that. And then she sees what is next most important and completes it. And so on. Whatever doesn't get done, doesn't get done, but at least the most important things do. It is so simple, and not necessarily easy, but it's really all we can do.

Mindfulness helps cultivate the *self-awareness* that tells us what the most important task is and teaches us how to listen to our body, heart, mind, and spirit. Furthermore, mindfulness can help us with *emotion regulation* to care for the strong feelings of excitement or fear that might come up with that task because it is so important. We can notice the feeling tone related to the task at hand, care for the emotion, and even harness the emotion's energy to complete the important task. And finally, mindfulness can help us with the *attention control* to bring our mind to focus on the particular important task, to be there fully for it (which may result in the negative emotions slipping away), and to complete it efficiently and in high quality.

Overall, mindfulness helps us see what is called for in our career paths, let go of attachment to what is perhaps not the best path and of aversion to difficult or unsavory elements, and then do what is needed to best match who we are and what the world requires. Through fostering an open body, heart, mind, and spirit, we can continue to do these career tasks while caring for ourselves and others along the way. Below is a meditation on career performance that you might like to try.

Work Performance Meditation

The intention of this meditation is to first ground yourself in your body, heart, mind, and spirit, and then direct your full self toward considering factors that may either be limiting or enhancing your performance at work. With curiosity and gentleness, by exploring and understanding the roots causes, often wise next steps can appear to improve your performance in work and indeed in life.

Inviting you to find your anchor, and then explore opening the body, heart, mind, and spirit.

What is here in your emotions around work?

What are your struggles? Inviting you to name them. For example, is it procrastination? Institutional racism? Income instability? Overwork? Burnout? Tensions with coworkers?

Whatever arises, if it is a strong emotion, inviting you to hold it as a parent would a crying child. Letting it settle.

Is there a root cause of that strong emotion?

Based on that root cause, what is a sensible next step?

If that next step brings strong emotions, holding them and looking for their roots.

Slowly over time (and sometimes suddenly) insights can arise, and you can use your skills of attention control, self-awareness, and emotion regulation to engage in the most important next step, even if it is difficult. Sometimes what seems like the most difficult step is actually quite easy once you get started.

Note that you can do a similar contemplation as above, but instead of looking at the struggles in your career, you can ask more appreciative self-reflection questions, such as: What is most fulfilling for me at work right now? In what tasks am I happiest? What activities have the biggest positive difference to my community? What arises in my thoughts, emotions, and physical sensations around what I could be doing to further foster my enjoyment, fulfilment, and impact at work?

And just see what insights arise from these questions and how they may apply to your career priority tasks in this moment.

Using Mindfulness to Enhance Your Life Path

As I mentioned in the introduction, Travis, after finishing his master's degree, had to decide whether he wanted to do a PhD with the goal of becoming a professor or to emphasize his creative life. Travis shared how mindfulness training allowed him to feel into the challenge, cut through the social pressure, and do what felt more wholesome.

Travis said, "I read a couple of books about death and started wondering, *When I'm on my death bed, what would I think about what I did in my life, and would I be okay with that choice?* I asked myself, *What activity would I be okay with failing as long as I tried?* I picked art and teaching, so that's what I did. I let go of the PhD and being a professor, which were goals that felt hollow. So here I am, where I basically work at a day care in the afternoon and tutor fifth and twelfth graders. I'm dedicating a lot of my life to making creative music and videos. I think that my practice helped me see that I am naturally someone who teaches kids and makes improvisational music and creative videos." Mindfulness helped Travis see who he naturally is, have the courage and skill to cut through what he perceived to be society's norms and pressures, and live a life that matches his skills and passions. He doesn't make as much money as he imagined he would, but he is happy, as are the kids that he cares for.

In thinking about your life and the path you want to take, what is it for you that fills you up? Is it friendships? Pottery? Reading wonderful literature? Making music? Caring for children? Dance? The beauty of each of us is that we are unique. Mindfulness can help increase our self-awareness to better understand who we are and to identify what fills us with wholesome joy, happiness. And fulfillment. What is it for you? Below is a contemplation that will guide you through exploring that for yourself; it is adapted from a practice used in Mindfulness-Based Cognitive Therapy (Segal et al. 2012).

Enhance Your Life Path Meditation

The intention of this mindfulness practice is to reflect on what fills you up and what drains you so you can bring the things that lead to happiness and well-being and let go of what doesn't in your life.

Taking a moment to ground yourself in your anchor point, of the breath, body, or sound. Then as you are ready, ask yourself the following questions. I invite you to answer in writing, creating a list that you can keep and refer back to.

What nourishes me?

In my life, what do I do that nourishes my health and happiness?

What do I do that makes me feel alive and well?

What are some things that I have found helpful or enjoyable that I can do more of?

How can I add nourishment to my life?

What is a nourishing activity that I can do every day this week?

What is a nourishing activity that I can do once this week?

What drains me?

In my life, what do I do that drains my health and happiness?

What do I do that makes me feel worse?

What are some things that I have found unhelpful or harmful that I can do less of?

How can I refrain from draining myself?

What is an unwholesome activity that I can avoid doing every day this week?

What is an unwholesome activity that I can avoid doing once this week?

Each of us will have different answers to the questions. For me, if my life includes close relationships; physical activity; healthy, tasty food; time in nature; creative expression, such as playing mandolin, gardening, or woodwork; time for meditative contemplation; and meaningful service to society, I'm good. In fact, when I do that, the quality and quantity of my work is higher. Whatever the factors are for you is fine, as they are based on your wisdom and experience.

Using Mindfulness to Improve Performance in Your Areas of Interest

Brumage and Gross (2015) described how mindfulness can help sports performance, enabling athletes to make choices of how to *respond skillfully*, instead of *reacting*, to challenging situations. For example, football players frequently make mistakes that result in turnovers and dropped passes. *Reacting* to the mistake, such as by shoving another player or getting caught up in one's head rerunning what happened, can result in a penalty or a further mistake by missing what is happening in the next play of the game. Instead, *responding skillfully* to the mistake—such as by bringing awareness and discernment to what in the mind and body is interfering with performance, then seeing what arises in the thoughts as a skillful response, and then acting on it with the body and mind—can enable the athlete to come into the present moment and focus on the task at hand. This can be similarly applied to a dance performance, music performance, or a creating a piece of art. The aim is to either respond and create something beautiful with what we have or realize it's okay and best to start over.

Let's try a meditation, if you like. (Note: An audio recording of this is on the website for this book, http://www.newharbinger.com/49135, if you want to listen to it.)

Life Performance Meditation

The intention of this meditation is to explore a particular area of your life that you would like to enhance your performance in. Directing your open body-heart-mind-spirit complex to the skill in real time, along with self-awareness, attention control, and emotion regulation, will allow you to be fully present, harnessing and focusing your wisdom to the skill that you would like to enhance performance in.

Bringing to mind an area of your life that you would like to perform better in.

Please be quite specific. Is it a particular class in which you'd like to do better academically? Is it a particular art form, like graphic design or metalwork? Perhaps athletics? Public speaking? Cooking? Calling to mind anything you would like to perform better in is fine.

What are your growth opportunities in it? As you call it up, being aware of your physical sensations, emotions, and thoughts related to this area you would like to enhance your performance in.

Imagining yourself actually doing that action, or preferably actually doing it.

Part of what allows us to perform well is bringing our whole selves to what we are engaged in.

So in this moment, while you are performing your chosen activity, what is your body, heart, mind, or spirit sharing?

In this way, we are unleashing our entire self and directing it to the area that we want to perform in, allowing our unique skills and perspectives to come through.

Speaking of directing, this is where the attention control comes in.

Inviting you to hold an open body, mind, heart, and spirit, directing them in this moment to this area of endeavor.

Another element in concentration is to be right here in this moment, where all you are doing is the task that you are focusing on improving your performance in.

Letting everything else go so you are here, now.

As we shift into the emotional regulation domain, our emotional tone around what we want to perform in is important. There might be strong emotions here if it's something we really care about—excitement, dread, fear of judgment, whatever. Touching into the emotional tone and seeing what's here. Caring for what is here, and if called for, letting go of superfluous thoughts, and coming back to the object of meditation, which in this case is doing the next step in the domain that you would like to enhance your performance in.

Continuing to work with two axes directed to your actions in the area you would like to perform:

(1) Opening your body, heart, mind, and spirit, and directing the messages from them to this area of performance in the moment while you are doing it.

(2) Using your skills in attention control, self-awareness, and emotion regulation to not only be aware of what is arising in yourself and surrounding, but also to channel them to perform in the way that only

you can in this area, in ways that are distinct from anyone else, and
beautifully you.

Travis, whom I mentioned above, makes improvisational music. He uses technical equipment to express himself, including a synthesizer and drum machines. There are many wires and points along the chain where things can go wrong, and that can be challenging. I asked him about the connection between his mind and body, and he said, "When you are in the zone, it feels like there is no resistance. It feels like the system is working in harmony. A metaphor is like shooting a gun or bow. There is a target, and I am hitting that target consistently. The intention and the motor expression of that intention are in harmony." By being self-aware and harnessing that awareness skillfully, Travis learned what it took to bring him into an open, expressive, and creative state and to express his creativity authentically, even if it isn't always easy.

There are many ways that mindfulness can influence performance, and the research on this area is just getting under way. I invite you to explore its effects on your performance for yourself. Through the lens of *self-awareness* of what your body and mind are sharing with you, see if you can leverage mindfulness to allow your true self to come through, to work with your attention control so you are 100 percent engaged in your activity. You can experiment with working with your skills of emotion regulation to notice what this area of performance brings up for you and to harness that energy like a sailor would harness the wind, while at the same time, caring for the strong emotions that arise, continuing to move forward, and performing at a higher level.

Social Media and Screen Use

We've all seen the studies and anecdotal evidence of about the challenges of social media and use of screens. Both are intentionally designed to be addictive. Sabrina shared, "I've noticed the effects of social media and technology in my life. I deleted my Instagram account as a result. My generation specifically really appreciates and glorifies extremely, extremely skinny women to an unhealthy point. And that gets shared as an echo chamber in social media. Every female I know has a problem with eating. Everyone has a thought disorder related to weight, eating, and body image. The 'ideal weight' is not healthy. A lot of girls will take extreme measures to make that goal."

Camille shared another challenge with the internet and social media: "We are bombarded with stimuli. It can also suck our time and energy. Finding a way to harness what is good about the internet and digital options, but leaving behind the noise and its incessive nature, is a huge challenge for young people."

And yet, screens and social media have transformed society in positive ways as well. For example, people from Dubai, Brazil, Florida, and Rhode Island can all be together in the same video conference, have meaningful conversations with each other, and learn deeply in ways that a book can't offer. Grandchildren can connect to grandparents across oceans. Stories and wisdom can be communicated powerfully through film. So it's clear that screens and social media can be tools that make life better. The challenge is avoiding the elements that make it worse.

As with all tools, we keep those that help us and let go of those that don't. We can determine if a particular digital tool is helpful with mindful awareness of our thoughts, emotions, and physical sensations. We can ask in a curious nonjudgmental way, "Is this digital tool helping in this moment more than anything else I can do?" If so, great. Continue using it. If not, let it go, and move onto the next highest priority action to take care of yourself and others.

Our relationship to screens and social media echoes how we deal with other potentially addictive products, like alcohol, sugar, and caffeine. Some people completely swear off social media, while others try to be aware of how it makes them feel and respond accordingly. There is no single right approach; the best approach is whatever works for you.

While there hasn't been much research on the effects of mindfulness training on social media addiction, one randomized controlled trial evaluated the effects of the mindfulness app Headspace along with self-monitoring of social media use and mood tracking. The study showed significant improvements in the smartphone distraction scale compared to the control group at the end of the ten-day intervention (Throuvala et al. 2020).

With these powerful digital tools, there are many opportunities to use *self-awareness* of our thoughts, emotions, and sensations, tapping into to what our body and mind are telling us about a tool. We can then use our *attention control* to bring our mind to where it's most useful to be in this moment, while caring for our *emotional well-being*, based on what the digital media is bringing into our mind and body.

Digital Media Meditation

The intention of this meditation is to leverage openings you have had in your body, heart, mind, and spirit coupled with developing your prowess in self-awareness, attention control, and emotion regulation. You can then direct those skills to digital media. This meditation is designed to improve your relationship with the useful and harmful elements of social media tools so you are grounded and free when using them.

I invite you to get a screen that you would like to explore your relationship with in a mindful way, such as your phone, tablet, laptop, or video game console.

Putting the device beside you, start with a meditation on an anchor point, such as the breath, body, or sound.

Exploring opening the body, heart, mind, and spirit; observing if any are closed, the roots of those closures; and seeing if there are ways to heal and transform those roots to foster openings to transpire.

Then pick up your device. Just hold it without turning it on.

What's arising in the thoughts, emotions, or physical sensations?

Is there craving or aversion, for example?

Can you be there with those experiences like a parent would be holding an upset child?

Just exploring your responses in a safe space. You can always put the device down if it is overwhelming.

What's here?

Now inviting you to put the device down again, as you practice attention control and self-awareness around devices, screens, and social media.

I'd now invite you to pick up your device and go to one of the apps, programs, or games that is decently challenging for you to limit your use of. As you open it, don't go any further than opening it. Pause there.

How does this feel in the body, mind, and heart?

What is a skillful next step?

Inviting you to engage with it for one minute and no longer. Remember, this is a meditation, so inviting you to be there with it and to be aware of your mind and body as you engage with it, knowing you can stop or redirect at any time. It's just a meditation. You might want to set a timer for a minute, if you think that will be helpful.

After a minute, once again practicing the self-awareness and attention control to turn it off and come back to your anchor point. Noticing where the mind is.

What thoughts are here? What emotions?

Allowing the mind to settle back into that anchor point.

As you sit with this experience, do any insights or awarenesses arise in your relationship with the use of this digital tool?

What ways are skillful for you to engage with it? What ways are less skillful?

Moving forward, would you like to commit to or experiment with any particularly skillful ways of using this device? If so, what are they?

I invite you to take action on what arose for you.

In this chapter, we leveraged your training from the first four chapters to open your body, heart, mind, and spirit to apply it to yourself. You applied it to your career, life's path outside of career, and relationship with screens and social media. In the next chapter, we will shift from applying these openings to yourself to applying them to your relationship with your environment, including your social, political, and physical environments.

Home Practices

1. This week, on most days, I invite you to begin with a mindfulness practice that fosters your concentration, such as focusing on the breath, body, or sound. Or maybe you would like to start with some mindful movement followed by a stationary concentration practice. Whatever your mind and body are telling you that will support you to get grounded and sets the conditions to open is fine. And then, check in with your body, heart, mind, and spirit to see if they are open, and if not, ask why not. Looking at the answer without judgment and not unnaturally forcing any openings (because you can't force them anyway).

2. I invite you, as we begin to come toward the end of this book, to consider offering yourself a daily mindfulness practice informed by the prior chapters of this book but adapted to you. Maybe that's starting with a focused attention meditation and then shifting to a physical activity meditation. Maybe it is a loving-kindness meditation.

When I asked my teacher Joanne Friday what her typical daily practice was, while she formally practiced meditation and mindfulness for about an hour each morning, she shared that she offered herself the practice that she most needed each day. Based on your experience of the different practices in this book, I encourage you to start to build a set of them that best serve you and your unique circumstances at this moment in time, and each day offer yourself a practice that would be of most benefit to you and those you serve.

CHAPTER 6

Practical Applications for Our Surroundings
Society and Environment

Social relationships can provide some of the most wonderful experiences and some of the most difficult ones. There is a reason this chapter is toward the end of the book. If there is anything that needs a strong foundation in mindfulness practice, it is our relationships with others.

Our relationship with the physical environment is similar in many ways. Evidence suggests that connection with the natural environment can be good for mental and physical health, as we will learn more about in this chapter. For those concerned about environmental degradation, climate change, species extinction, and other issues facing the natural world, it is also helpful to stay grounded in mindful awareness as we engage skillfully in actions to nurture the natural environment.

This chapter harnesses your training in attention control, self-awareness, and emotion regulation and will show you how to direct it toward your relationships with others and the physical environment. The goal is to leverage personal strengths to respond powerfully and authentically to the needs of society and the environment. By matching your skills and interests with the greatest needs of society and the planet, as well as strengthening communication with other people, you can become more self-expressed— doing important work while taking care of yourself in the process.

Social Environment

Amelia, a young adult who went through one of my mindfulness courses shared, "My best friend, Ella, and I have been really close since our freshman year of college. It wasn't until I started meditating and becoming more mindful of my relationships that I realized I wasn't fully appreciating my relationship with her. When we were hanging out, I was taking those times for granted. I would be on my phone or talking about myself and not fully present. I would not be fully there for the conversation, not focused on what she was saying and how she was feeling. Our conversations were stifled because of that. I can say confidently now because being more mindful of these things, I recognized that Ella is my best friend and going to be in my life forever, and if I care for her like that, I need to express that to her and treat her the way she deserves. I set that intention for myself. Now I deliberately make sure I am making eye contact with her, being mindful of the conversation, and being mindful of myself too. If I have a random thought, I notice that thought, know that I am in conversation with Ella right now, and come back to it. Since then, I have noticed my relationship with her become a lot stronger. It has more depth to it, and our conversations get better every time."

Amelia went on to share how mindfulness affected her relationship with a parent. "With my mom, I can be extremely reactive. I am generally not a judgmental person, but when speaking with my mom, I am. With her, everything she says just riles me up. With my improved emotional regulation and self-awareness because of my mindfulness practice, I am more aware of the fact that I am reactive and that I immediately jolt when she says something. Now that I am more aware of that, I see the emotions more objectively. It has improved my relationship with her. Now, when I am with her, I am calmer, less reactive."

In bringing her attention control to be present with Ella, her self-awareness to notice how she is feeling when engaging with others, and fostering her emotional regulation, especially when talking with her mom, Amelia saw improvements in many of her relationships.

Another way mindfulness serves us in relationships is in helping us notice biases toward others, such as those related to race, gender, age, disability status, or intellectual capacity. Sometimes we aim biases toward others; other times biases are directed toward us. Some of us receive far more discrimination than others. For example, My Ngoc shared how mindfulness and meditation training have helped her process a lot of her own internalization of marginalization and trauma. It has helped her become more aware of her own body sensations and identify racial aggressions. From that, she has been able to recognize sooner when she is uncomfortable with situations. She has been able to let herself cry more easily including in front of others. That has been helpful rather than hiding.

My Ngoc did an internship in with a social work organization. In the past, she had worked with organizations that actively cared for underserved populations. This placement was different in who it served and the diversity of its staff. During the orientation, the staff talked about their identities, and My Ngoc was aware that she and one other woman were the only people of color. The two of them shared their racial identity, and no one who was white did. My Ngoc expressed discomfort with her supervisor the second time they met about the lack of openness and discussion about diversity in the staff. My Ngoc noticed it was building up in herself, and she recognized and articulated that it was something that she had been thinking about.

Because of her mindfulness practice helping her become more aware of how she was feeling, she started the conversations immediately. She said it felt productive and that she was able to take action. She learned it wasn't the first time that the lack of discussion on diversity and inclusion was raised with that organization. As a result, while the organization didn't change the way it addressed diversity and inclusion, My Ngoc's supervisor encouraged her do more advocacy work with community groups to get a more rewarding internship experience.

While she continued her work with this organization, My Ngoc's mindfulness practice helped her work with feelings of craving and aversion. She learned that she had been craving a certain experience. She became aware that she did not need to be so averse to a field placement that was not the best place for her. When she did work with the organization, she became better at resting in her body and grounding herself through every meeting. It allowed her to pay attention to the meaningful work that was there. She also realized the kinds of organizations that would be a better fit as her career moved forward. In fact, in part through the clarity that came from that internship, she will soon be starting a PhD in social work dedicated to racial diversity and trauma.

When applying mindfulness to our biases toward others, we can use the mindfulness tools we have been learning in the book. For example, we can use nonjudgmental *self-awareness* to be more aware of the biases we have and how they are expressed. We also develop our *emotion regulation* (following the framework in figure 1.1) so we can be more comfortable with being uncomfortable. This can include, for example, going through antiracism and antisexism trainings and engaging in dialogue with groups both of our own affiliation and of those who often face discrimination with an open heart, body, mind, and spirit. As a result, we can invite more diverse cultures and perspectives into our lives, thereby allowing our wisdom to grow. And, by using our *attention control* training, we can act on what we know are best practices, whether it is to say something when we detect discrimination or to act in antidiscriminative ways.

The applications of mindfulness to our relationships with people are endless. We can also apply it when we feel there not enough people we are close to in our lives, specifically when we feel lonely.

As my student Lara shared, "I think one of the biggest things is isolation and lack of real social connection (even before the pandemic)." Our MBC randomized controlled trial showed that people who practice mindfulness experienced significantly reduced loneliness (figure 6.1), as have most of the (relatively few) other mindfulness randomized controlled trials. It seems that mindfulness training may help reduce loneliness in a few ways: (1) With the in-person mindfulness practice and training groups, it creates opportunities for meaningful conversations and friendships to grow outside of class. (2) Our time alone becomes a more a contemplative experience (for example, just being there with your full experience of the mind, body, heart, and spirit while washing the dishes) so while we may not have more social contacts, the feelings of loneliness can subside. (3) Mindfulness training may foster more prosocial skills, such as the STOP practice, so we are more likely to pause before reacting in a way that could damage a relationship, thereby making us more enjoyable to be around. An example contemplative practice applied to social relationships is shown below if you'd like to try it out.

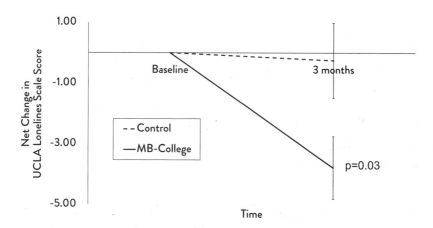

Figure 6.1   Changes in loneliness (UCLA Loneliness Scale score) from the beginning to the end of the college term. Participants were randomized to (1) Mindfulness-Based College or (2) the control group that received mental health services if needed and waited to take the course until the following term.

Relationships Mindfulness Practice

The intention of this meditation is to engage in a mindful communication and listening practice not only with yourself but also with another person. Communication with others can be one of the more challenging areas to apply mindfulness and one of the most important areas. This meditation gives you a resource to support your ability to access your inner wisdom moment by moment when communicating with others.

Taking a moment to remember if there was a time when you felt fully heard and understood. Perhaps a time when you were with someone who just "got" you. Bringing to mind where you were, what your surroundings were, and who was there.

As you call up that time in your mind, noticing what was happening in the body during that time. What physical sensations were manifesting?

And how about emotions?

What feelings were present while you were feeling heard and understood by this person, or people?

What thoughts were going through your mind while that event was happening?

And what is being felt in the physical sensations, emotions, and thoughts now as you reflect on that time of being heard and understood?

Imagine yourself reflecting in your own words, what you just noticed, as if you were summarizing it.

Inviting you this week, to pick someone and ask them the question above (for example, "Tell me about a time that you felt really heard and understood, and what was going on in your mind and body when that happened.")

Or pick another question.

And then just listen, without interrupting.

Noticing what arises in your emotions and thoughts in the process, as that conversation is a meditation in and of itself. It's just with another person, in relationship.

And then, as they finish, reflect in your own words what they shared, and ask if that understanding was right. Then if you like, share with them how their sharing made you feel or what it brought up in you.

As Joanne Friday used to share, "Can we listen without having an opinion?"

So often when we listen, we are thinking about what we are going to say next or trying to think of something interesting related to what that person is sharing.

Try to just listen and then reflect what you heard.

In that process, there is a good chance that they will feel really heard and understood and in turn give you the opportunity to be as well.

This is an important way to bring mindfulness to where the rubber meets the road—to our relationships with others.

Inviting you this week to bring mindful awareness to your sensations, emotions, and thoughts while keeping an open body, heart, mind, and spirit when interacting with others. This is a tall order, so be sure to care for yourself in the process, working to be in the comfort or growth zones (but not overwhelmed zone). Even moving a little more in the direction of being fully present in relationships can have sizable changes in the quality of our relationships.

Political Environment

Because mindfulness helps us see clearly and free ourselves from unhelpful biases, it can also be useful in supporting our communities and our relationship with the political environment. Mindfulness can help us take a step back from what the media, special interest groups, and lobbyists are asking us to consider so we can look at the big picture of the greatest needs. Doing so can allow us to include those who do not have the power or privilege to lobby and discover how governance could best serve everyone. It can inform the actions we take, including who we vote for and our own political actions. It can also help free us from dichotomous ways of thinking, even about which political party is "right" or "wrong" and instead be open to new perspectives with an open body, mind, heart, and spirit.

A young adult named Paul shared that mindfulness training help him express himself when the time is right. "I learned that I don't need to take my beliefs so seriously. I can have halfway intelligent political conversations with people who feel strongly on either side. That illustrates how I feel about mindfulness in communication—not to get too attached to a particular viewpoint. I am more able to go into a conversation willing to listen and to ask myself, *Where is this person coming from? What experiences have they had to lead them to say that thing they just said to me?*"

Our engagement with the political environment can bring up strong emotions and thoughts. Mindfulness training allows us not only to become more aware of them, but also to hold and care for them in skillful ways, noticing what arises in ourselves and taking the skillful next steps. For example, we can offer loving-kindness to political representatives, which can then translate into action. Joanne Friday would frequently write what she called "love letters" to political representatives, thanking them for their service, sharing her perspectives on what was needed in the governance system, and asking them clear questions about how they plan to manage challenges arising in the population. In doing so, it was her practice to stay open and grounded, while still taking action whether it was through letter writing, phone calls to government officials, or participating in political demonstrations. There are many examples of actions that can be taken in political areas informed by mindfulness practices. One of the best examples in the United States is Congressman Tim Ryan of Ohio, who wrote the book entitled *Healing America*. He introduced mindfulness training to the House Well-Being Office and supported its use in schools across America.

Jamie Bristow leads the Mindfulness Initiative, which is a policy institute and think tank in the United Kingdom. It supports an all-party parliamentary group that works at the interface between science and policy to introduce evidence-based mindfulness programs, such as Mindfulness-Based Cognitive Therapy, to members of the public in the UK. The politicians' physical and mental well-being is also supported through mindfulness programs open to members of all political parties.

Below is a mindfulness practice applied to our relationship with the political environment.

Relationship with Politics Meditation

The intention of this meditation is to offer loving-kindness toward yourself and others, with an emphasis on freeing yourself from grasping and unskillful ways of thinking, offering loving-kindness to those engaged in politics, and taking wise action where you are called to do so.

> *Inviting you to find a position that allows you to get grounded and centered, perhaps starting by connecting to your anchor point of the breath, body, or sound. As your concentration comes more into the present moment and more connected to the body and mind, offering yourself the contemplations below.*
>
> *May I be well in body, heart, mind, and spirit.*
>
> *May I know how to nurture joy in myself every day.*
>
> *May I be free from attachment and aversion, but not be indifferent. In other words, may I be free from grasping to certain ways of thinking or acting that are unskillful.*
>
> *However, upon learning what is skillful and kind for myself and the world, may I take action where it is called for.*
>
> *Now considering a public figure, such as a political member whom you have respect and appreciation for, offering to them:*
>
> *May this person be well in body, heart, mind, and spirit.*
>
> *May they know how to nurture joy in themselves every day.*

May this person be free from attachment and aversion, but not be indifferent.

Continue to offer this loving-kindness now to a public figure, such as a politician whom you feel more neutral toward, noticing what arises in the sensations, emotions, and thoughts as you do so.

Moving on to consider a public figure whom you have difficulty with. Caring for yourself in the process, offering the contemplations above to this person.

It can sometimes be helpful when offering loving-kindness to people we have difficulty with to blend it with understanding and compassion. For example, imagine that challenging politician as a seven-year-old child. What would it have been like to grow up as that person, and what were the influences on them, such as from parents or the surrounding community? We can foster compassion for politicians, as they have difficult and often thankless jobs as they work to serve their communities while being publicly scrutinized.

Widening out to include all people, or all beings, offering the contemplations above.

Now, taking a moment to reflect on what arises within you about ways you could change things for the better in your community or country.

The nation is a collection of values, and those who are most engaged with the political process are more likely to have their values listened to and acted upon. Chances are you have values that would benefit your school, neighborhood, town, city, nation, and continent.

What would be a skillful next step here?

I invite you to take it.

As the meditation comes toward a close, inviting you to take a moment to return to your anchor point of the breath, body, or sound to get grounded as you transition to the next steps in your day.

Physical Environment

The physical environment includes places such as our home, work, neighborhood, town, or city and even country. There's certainly a lot that could be covered about bringing mindfulness to our relationship with our physical environments. In this book, I will focus on the home environment and the natural environment, but lessons from these applications can extend to other environments as well.

Home Environment

Our home space is in many ways a perfect place to get creative and explore the nuances of our individual practice and preferences. This is true even if it is just your bedroom or, as the case of my daughters who share a room, the side of the room where you sleep. The physical environment we spend time in impacts our well-being and what we think about. We can use mindful awareness to notice how and then craft the environment to foster conditions to help us be happy and healthy, succeed in our highest priorities, and build the life we would like.

Philosopher and Zen Buddhist scholar Shin'ichi Hisamatsu (1982) proposed esthetic principles that we can use to weave mindfulness in with our home environment in ways that hold promise to improve our health and happiness. Hisamatsu's principals were designed for art but can be applied to aesthetics in our home environment whether it is two-dimensional art, furniture, a garden, or the way we set the table for dinner. Professor Tim Lomas linked these Zen aesthetic principles to well-being (Lomas et al. 2017). Using the mindfulness skill of self-awareness about your physical sensations, emotions, and thoughts, you are invited to try each principal on for size, and see which, if any, resonate with you the most. If some do resonate, I invite you to craft your home environment to include those principles, many of which can often be done even without spending money. See what you think of the list below.

1. *Simplicity*. This is beauty in being sparse and without clutter. It is the omission of the nonessential. Meditation often creates an uncluttered mind. An uncluttered mind can then create an uncluttered home, and vice versa. For example, you see a gift that someone gave you. While it is a sign of their love and you can appreciate it, maybe you realize that it doesn't really resonate with you. You could decide to pass it on to someone who may appreciate it more. Letting go of clutter and nonessential items in our home can be liberating and free us from visual reminders that bring us down while creating space for the visual elements that raise us up. Also, it is a way to work with craving for material items, as we can see if they really bring happiness. In doing so, we not only foster happiness and well-being but also save our money to use toward things that bring happiness.

2. *Asymmetry*. This concept encourages features such as being gnarled, irregular, or sweeping. Indeed, we ourselves are irregular, and that is what makes us unique and who we are. Not to mention the world is asymmetrical. This is an opportunity to bring the world as it is into our home and be connected to it and to ourselves, just as we are. For example, as I step into my twin daughters' bedroom, there are string lights winding their way around the room, a beautiful plant hanging in the window on one side of the room, and a cozy window-front reading nook on the other with blankets careening around the cushion. The asymmetry they created gives it almost a nature-like, authentic feel that is comfortable, and I am drawn to it. Perhaps notice if there is asymmetry your environment, and if so, how it feels to you. Are there opportunities for more that would foster your happiness or well-being?

3. *Austere sublimity*. This concept is also called "lofty dryness" (obviously). It has qualities such as being aged, seasoned, cracked,

wind-dried, decayed, or weathered. Do you have an item from your ancestors in your home, that while it's maybe not the prettiest thing ever, there is some reason you keep it? That reason may be not only the sentimental value, but also in how having aged items in your home or yard make you feel. It doesn't cost anything to bring that old, twisted piece of wood home that you found at the beach or in the forest, but it may add an element of *austere sublimity* to your home.

The austere sublimity concept suggests that we be comfortable with impermanence or aging. We get old and die, as do our loved ones. Our material items usually get old and weathered. By having aged items in our home, it is a reminder of that so we can come to accept and embrace that nature and appreciate the character that age and weatheredness brings.

4. *Naturalness.* This concept refers to not being strained in producing an outcome and having no intent. It occurs when you are so fully in sync with the process of creating that there is no conscious effort in producing it. It has similarities to being in a flow state. And so, when creating your home or yard, what is it that naturally comes through you? How can you release your natural expression, and flow state, to craft your home for what you need and want it to be now, given your and your roommate's life now rather than how it was two years ago or how you imagine it to be in the future? While the term "naturalness" may sound like it refers to an item from nature, it refers to the naturalness in expression of your aesthetics. In other words, can you let your true self flow out into your home, creating aesthetics that are naturally expressing who you are and what you value?

5. *Freedom from attachment.* This brings in an essence of freeing ourselves from habit or inviting in the unconventional. We can often be attached to objects, but we can also be attached

to unhealthy habits that our home environment supports. Say for example that you struggle with addiction to alcohol and there is a shelf displaying alcohol in your home. That shelf may remind you of a habit that has become unhealthy, so you decide to replace it with something health promoting. Maybe it is writing a love note to your special person and placing it on the breakfast table for them to find. Or perhaps it is lighting a fire on a cold winter morning. Or, in the case of my friend Damian, a ten-foot-high tent with an assortment of seating in the backyard and hand-woven ropes through the trees to create a massive spiderweb-like hammock to hang out in. Is there a way to embody mindfulness to free yourself from your habitual patterns or attachments by bringing something into your home or yard that is fresh and real in this moment?

6. *Tranquility*. This concept is related to quiet and calm and being inwardly focused. If tranquility, or being free from turbulent emotions, is something you value, then you can provide elements in your home and yard that promote that. Perhaps it is the type of music you play in the morning as you start your day or the kind of art that you hang on the walls. It may be the plants that you select. With mindful awareness, notice how the physical environment of your home makes you feel, and if you want to foster more tranquility, consider what elements you would like to remove or bring in that foster feelings of peace and well-being.

7. *Subtle profundity* or *deep reserve*. This can be considered an element that represents the depths of existence and how that is beyond intellectual understanding. A Zen koan that taps into this concept is, "What is *this* which can't be named or intellectually known?"

What is the mysterious suchness of all things? And how can you bring that into your home? Perhaps it is a figure that represents your religion or a picture of a wise person in your life. As Lomas shares, it represents an element of "being moved to the core of one's being, without quite knowing why" (Lomas et al. 2017). What is already in your home or yard that does that for you, if there is something that does? Would you like to search for something that does? It is for you to discover and decide and notice the effects on your life.

We are often fed information ("Buy this." "Consume that.") that doesn't make us happier in a long-term way. It may bring excitement but not happiness. These seven aesthetic principles have much wisdom but little penetrance in the west. They may bring longer-term happiness and then allow you to skillfully navigate life by not biting the many fishhooks dangling in our social and physical environments that don't bring well-being. According to Hisamatsu (1982), they were mostly focused in China, Korea, and Japan during the seventh to the fifteenth centuries. The contemplation below lets you try them on for size and see which, if any, bring happiness and well-being into your life.

Physical Environment Meditation

The intention of this meditation is to bring self-awareness of the impact of the seven aesthetic principles on our physical sensations, emotions, and thoughts to see which, if any, could have positive effects on our well-being and happiness.

Taking a moment to focus your attention on an object that grounds you, such as the breath, body, or sound.

Then, as you are ready, checking in with the body, heart, mind, and spirit. Are they open? If not, why not?

Inviting you to come into the present moment, aware of the body, thoughts, and emotions.

Inviting you to bring to mind the seven aesthetic principles and seeing what ones most resonate with you, if any.

Perhaps asking which one(s) you would most like to bring more into your home environment.

As a reminder, the principals are:

simplicity

asymmetry

austere sublimity

naturalness

freedom from attachment

tranquility

subtle profundity.

What arises in your emotions, thoughts, and physical sensations as you consider these principals and how they apply to the home you live in?

If you are in your home, inviting you to mindfully walk around it (either physically or mentally bringing it to mind) and noticing through the senses of sight, sound, smell, and touch what is here?

How does it feel?

What is the quality of your emotions and thoughts as you consider this physical environment? How does it support the well-being of your body, mind, heart, and spirit?

Is there any desire for action that arises that you are considering taking?

Perhaps it is removing something in your home that brings you down or introducing something in that lifts you up. Maybe it is considering one or more of the seven elements that you would like to bring into your space more.

Inviting you in the coming minutes, hours, or days to make the change(s) in your home environment.

As you finish the contemplation, inviting you to take a moment and come back to your anchor point, grounding into this moment and to this body, heart, mind, and spirit as you transition to the next part of your day or evening.

While I appreciate and incorporate Hisamatsu's seven principals into my home, I like to add a few additional elements: social connection, food, warmth, and coziness—all of which fit into the concept of "hygge." Meik Wiking, CEO of the Happiness Research Institute in Copenhagen, Denmark, wrote the New York Times best-selling book, *The Little Book of Hygge: The Danish Way to Live Well.* Hygge (pronounced "hoogah," "hhyooguh," or possibly "heurgh") has qualities of coziness and comfort that bring feelings of contentment and well-being. It often includes contentment from simple pleasures, such as such as togetherness with friends and family, comfort foods and drinks, warmth, soft lighting, cozy clothing, harmony, and present-moment awareness.

There are many elements that foster hygge. Some include candlelight, gathering with a few close friends or being outside in nature and then coming home to a warm bowl of soup. Other examples are blankets, wearing homemade socks, and possibly having a cup of hot chocolate or other treat. Watching movies gets a thumbs-up, especially if done with a loved one or friend, while sipping tea with a storm raging outside. It could be a summer picnic with homemade food and drinks. Being here in the present moment is emphasized with hygge. Much of what's hygge doesn't really cost anything extra; it's just a matter of emphasizing it in our lives or at least trying it on for size and seeing how it feels. You may be in a dorm room, a studio apartment, or possibly your parents' basement, but consider what elements you could add to promote happiness. The intersection of mindfulness with this is creating conditions in your home that bring well-being and happiness can also encourage you to be "here" in this moment. The next section will shift to exploring conditions outside our home that can foster happiness and health, specifically the natural environment.

Natural Environment

When I was in my twenties, my dad treated me to a trip up in the Peace River area of British Columbia, Canada, in the foothills of the Rocky Mountains where few people live. We took all-terrain vehicles along a rough trail for miles, ending up at a small home with several horses. The next day, we embarked with the guide on a several-day horseback ride through low scrub bush from valley to valley, over ridges, and never seeing a sign of humans, other than the path we traveled. As we worked our way into a valley to set up camp for the evening, the large animals moved out of that valley. In the evenings, I would walk, often on my own, up to a ridge with binoculars, and look into the valley on the other side. I saw caribou, elk, moose, and bison. One morning, as we were breaking camp, a grizzly bear a couple hundred yards away broke into a run. The muscles rippled under her fur. It was a beautiful sight as she ran into a cluster of trees behind our camp. I didn't need coffee to help with present-moment awareness as we packed up camp, keeping an eye on the trees behind us.

As we spent days in the wilderness, there was much about it that brought me into the moment and also gave me the space to step back and look at my life from a distance, noticing where I wanted to go next in my life's journey. I was struggling at the time, having gone straight into college and then into seven years of grad school, never taking a break from school since kindergarten. My heart and mind knew I didn't want to be doing pharmacology research on animals for the rest of my career, which is what my PhD was steering me toward. I had close friends, a girlfriend who was not a great fit for me, and the pressures of finding a career that was a good match for who I was. Taking a week to remove myself from those pressures and be in nature with my dad and others, surrounded by awe-inducing nature was exactly the recipe to process a lot of what needed to be. During that phase, I realized that I was growing up, taking control of my life and building it to be what I wanted. I ended up changing my career direction and breaking up with that girlfriend. In time, I met my long-term romantic partner, Betsy, knowing in my body, heart, mind, and spirit that we are a good fit for each other. Being in nature provided the restoration that my body and mind needed, setting me up for better decisions to build the life of my dreams.

Indeed, the "attention restoration theory" (Bratman et al. 2012) invites us to maximize four elements that contribute to psychological restoration that are usually experienced in nature, shown in the sidebar. The invitation is to try these on for size and see which, if any, help your mind to rest and recover, perhaps building resilience for your day or weeks ahead.

The Four Elements of Attention Restoration Theory

Attention restoration theory proposes that exposure to nature brings enjoyment, improves focus, and enhances our ability to concentrate through these four elements:

1. *Extent*. Being fully immersed in the natural landscape is much more challenging in urban areas than doing so on a wilderness trip. But it's possible, and many people are working to make it easier. Take Frederick Law Olmstead for example. Olmstead designed many acclaimed city parks in the United States, including Central Park in New York City, and worked to create areas where all that was seen was nature. You can find ways to play around with this, even at the micro level looking at images of nature on a screen (shown in research studies to be of benefit; Bratman et al 2012) or having plants in your home or office. Or at the macro level, it could be going to a city park regularly or perhaps finding an opportunity to go for a hike in more of a wilderness setting.

2. *Being away.* This is about stepping away from day-to-day experiences and concerns, whether it is a small experience, like gazing out a window, or big one, like a multiday wilderness

experience. As my story above showed, getting away can make a big difference. But a shorter time can work too. For example, Bratman and colleagues (2015) randomly assigned participants to walk for almost an hour either in a natural or an urban environment. Participants who were assigned to the natural walk showed decreased anxiety, rumination, and negative mood along with increased positive mood and working memory performance, compared with participants who walked in an urban environment.

3. *Fascination.* Fascination naturally engages our attention without any effort on our part. This fascination, or what some people refer to as awe, can allow us to have that break and be inspired by the beauty of life, whether it is a blooming flower, a swallow streaking across a blue sky, or a mountain cresting in the distance.

4. *Compatibility.* Compatibility refers to how well the nature experience matches what we actually like about nature. For example, some of us prefer vegetable gardens, ocean beaches, mountains, or sipping coffee in front of the orchid on our plant stand. There are also cultural compatibilities and safety considerations, along with what is a fit with your background comfort with nature.

Finding ways to maximize the four elements of extent, being away, fascination, and compatibility may provide a nice break for you, giving perspective and rest.

The research on the effects of nature experience is building sizably, including in young adults. It was shown that when young people, particularly students, have a view of green spaces during school, they performed better on attention tests and stress recovery (Li and Sullivan 2016). A systematic review and meta-analysis of twenty-five nature-based mindfulness interventions in almost three thousand participants showed significant improvements in the overall combined psychological, physiological, and interpersonal effects. It seems that the type of nature experience had an effect, where natural environments characterized as forests or wild nature showed larger effects than environments characterized as gardens or parks (Djernis et al. 2019). Overall, evidence suggests that nature experience is good for our minds and bodies.

With the increasing movement toward cities, many of us are becoming disconnected with nature, not always considering the impacts of our actions on the natural environment, resulting in challenges, such as climate change. Mindfulness can help us become more aware of our actions and their impacts. It can help direct our attention toward actions that care for the environment and help us emotionally regulate when we are faced with environmental challenges, such as the increasing ramifications of climate change.

Lauren, who went through MBC, shared how she used mindfulness to help support her during a climate change-related catastrophe. "It's very personal to me in Louisiana. We are losing a football field of land every hour. My hometown was destroyed by two hurricanes this year (2020). Hurricane Laura hit Lake Charles at the beginning of the MBC course. I went to provide aid. It was very hard to see, and I experienced quite a degree of trauma. Learning the skills that I was given in the course were very helpful to process through that trauma."

Our relationship with the natural environment can happen in about as many ways as there are people in the world. In some ways, just by being part of the earth, we are in relationship with the natural environment. In coming to understand it and be cognizant that we're nurtured by it, my hope is that it will help us support and care for nature and in turn reduce our impact on it, including in ways that contribute to climate change. Below are a couple of self-reflections on bringing mindful awareness to nature.

Nature Experience Meditation

The intention of this meditation is to bring mindful self-awareness of your thoughts, emotions, and physical sensations to experience the four elements of attention restoration theory (extent, being away, fascination, and compatibility) and see if they do indeed bring you happiness and refresh your focus while observing if insights arise around bringing them more into your life or appreciating how you already do.

Inviting you to ground yourself in your anchor point of the breath, body, or sound.

As you are ready, inviting you to bring an element of nature into your view, such as a stone, a houseplant, a picture of nature that you find on the internet, or even preferably physically going into nature, such as into a backyard or park.

As you bring your awareness to your thoughts, emotions, and physical sensations as you invite nature into your view, how does it feel? Do certain objects or spaces promote more positive thoughts, emotions, or physical sensations than others? If so, what are they? That's good information.

Play around with the four elements, as follows:

Extent: For example, can you bring the nature close in around you (even getting closer to the houseplant, arranging many in one area, or going deeper into a forest or onto an ocean)?

Being away: Inviting you to step away from your day-to-day experience and concerns through instead being with this nature experience, just for this moment.

Fascination: Allowing the environment to naturally engage your attention, to fascinate you, without any effort on your part.

Compatibility: Finding a natural setting to be with in this moment that, while bringing awareness to your physical sensations, emotions, and thoughts, fills you up in some way that matches who you are.

As you are aware of the thoughts, emotions, and sensations arising within this nature experience, are there any next steps you want to take to foster nature experience more in your life or the lives of others?

Is there anything the arises in you related to your relationship with nature?

If so, inviting you to jot it down so you can bring any fruitful elements that arose in your contemplation more into your life in the coming days, weeks, and months.

This chapter focused on bringing our skills in self-awareness, attention control, and emotion regulation, coupled with an open body, heart, mind, and spirit, to our relationship with the social, political, physical, and natural environments. Doing so not only brings mindful awareness to our relationships with them but encourages us to take wise actions that express who we are. It allows us to be stewards of our environments during the brief period we are here on earth in this form while enjoying the wonders that our environments provide and helping ensure it will continue to support happy and healthy lives for beings seven generations in the future and beyond. In the final chapter, we will work on synthesizing these teachings, and I'll send you on your way with a toolkit that will support you to succeed, boost your well-being, and build the life you want.

Home Practices

1. Similar to the prior chapter, this week, on most days, I invite you to begin with a mindfulness practice that fosters your concentration, such as focusing on the breath, body, or sound, or maybe you would like to start with some mindful movement followed by a still concentration practice. Do whatever suits your mind and body, helps you get grounded, and sets the conditions to open. And then, check in to see if your body, heart, mind, and spirit are open, and if not, why not. Look at the response without judgment

and without unnaturally forcing any openings (because you can't unnaturally force any anyway).

Then as you are ready, direct your self-awareness toward your relationship with society and the environment, including your social environment, such as friendships, classmates, work relationships, family relationships; your political environment; the physical environment in your home (for example considering Hisamatsu's Zen esthetic principles or the hygge principles), yard, neighborhood, city or town, state, and country; as well as the natural environment. Can you use your attention control to be there with that important element of your social, political, physical, or natural environment and explore it using your self-awareness, as if you are seeing it for the first time with fresh eyes, an open mind, an open heart, and maybe even an open spirit? Can you engage with it using the mindfulness qualities of curiosity, nonjudgment, and self-kindness?

As you are there with what arises, what are the roots of the challenges with this social, political, natural, or physical environmental factor, or what are the roots of what gives joy and happiness in this area of your life because of that environmental influence? Can you harness the understanding of those roots to plot out a skillful next step, or a series of steps, forward that would be of benefit to you and perhaps all living beings?

2. Continue to build a daily practice that is customized to you. What are practices in other domains of your life outside of this book (for example spiritual traditions or self-care practices you know work for you even if they aren't mentioned here) that you know also make life better when you do them? Inviting you to create a daily personal practice this week that weaves together what you have learned in this book and outside this book that you know helps set you up for a good day, and a healthier, happier life.

CHAPTER 7

Sewing the Pieces Together

Humans have found methods to live healthily and happily for millennia. It's just that now the applications are unique in many ways to this time in history (for example to our relationships with digital media, processed foods, new pandemics, and climate change). We are at new frontiers, and I believe mindfulness is a fundamental tool to help with all of it. I hope that in the prior chapters, you discovered mindfulness practices that support your skills in self-awareness, attention control, and emotional regulation and can apply them to the biggest priorities in your life.

As Paul shared, "When I think about mindfulness applied to career choices or athletic choices, or anything, it's all one and the same for me." Paul, who dropped out of high school, was in and out of psychiatry wards, attempted suicide multiple times, and found himself in what he called "big boy's jail" by the time he was nineteen, found that mindfulness and meditation were the way out of these problems. A Buddhist nun visited him in jail and provided him with meditation and mindfulness training, which he applied regularly, including during a stint in solitary confinement.

After Paul was released, he attended various meditation and mindfulness communities and continued to practice. He shared, "I learned that you get good at falling; you get intimate with the ground. In some ways, mindfulness for me was an against-the-grain approach to access who I wanted to be. The autopilot of going along with social norms just led to more pain." Paul attended community college for graphic design with plans to apply to art school. He showed so much promise that he received numerous scholarship offers, including one from a top art school in the United States. He went for it.

Paul shared, "A lot of mindfulness practice might seem like refraining from the mindset of 'I have to be this good little boy and only water the wholesome seeds.' It's cleaning away the bullshit and what's not helpful so I can embrace and swim around in *what is* important. So I decided to go to art school and do this thing. That was twelve years ago. I finished art school and married someone who has similar values. Having a visual creative practice nourishes both our spirits, so we make time for it. I feel like the world doesn't support that. The world doesn't really support having a reflective, mindful approach to living. Sometimes slamming on the brakes is what is required. Stopping and asking myself: What the fuck am I doing? What is the point of all this? That sounds a little rough around the edges—but it's skillful irreverence."

"There is no shortage of pain." Paul went on to say. "It's not as though tragedy and loss don't happen. If I can be present, they don't sting quite as bad. They're still there, just not quite as loud. One of my favorite things about mindfulness is it can hold everything. I don't have to be just sad. I can be sad and content at the same time. I can be frustrated and content at the same time. It took a lot of practice to realize, 'Yeah, my blood is boiling. There's good and bad. They are both here.'"

Although he had a difficult start to life, his family was mostly on welfare, his parents divorced, and he experienced mental health challenges, Paul is now a mindfulness practitioner, and is training to become an MBSR and MBC instructor. He has systematically become aware of his body, heart, mind, and spirit, and knit those awarenesses together in his relationships with his career, life path, social media, politics, and other people in his life. That is what this chapter is about. When knitting a sweater, we knit the front, back, and sleeve segments separately. And then we join those segments to create the complete garment to put on, wear, and be protected from the elements, and go out into the world and do what is called for. This chapter is designed to join the prior chapters together and leave you not only with cohesive understanding, but the inspiration to act on that understanding.

As shown in figure 7.1, this book provides training in concentration and self-awareness focused on different parts, like opening the body, opening the heart (emotions), opening the mind (thoughts), and opening the spirit (nature of reality). The training then invites us to apply those openings to our lives (such as our career, life path, performance, and relationships with screens and social media) and our surroundings (including our social environment, political environment, and physical environment). This chapter weaves them all together so you have a cohesive framework, or a resilience "sweater" to wear, that will foster well-being for the rest of your life in yourself and in those whose lives you touch.

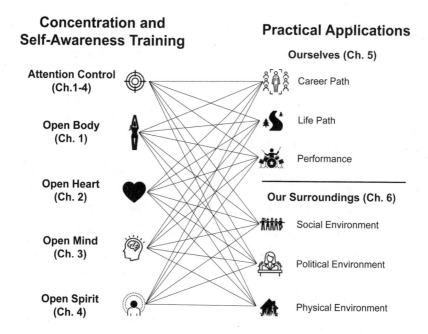

Figure 7.1 This book provides training in concentration (attention control) and self-awareness focused on opening the body (chapter 1), heart (emotions, chapter 2), mind (thoughts, chapter 3), and spirit (nature of reality, chapter 4). It then invites you to apply those openings to yourself (for example in your career, life path, performance, and relationships with screens and social media, chapter 5) and your surroundings (social environment, political environment, and physical environment, chapter 6). You can then weave them together so you have a cohesive framework to foster well-being for the rest of your life and for those whose lives you touch.

In the first, and last, class of MBC, we show figure 1.1, which basically maps out a path from mindfulness to well-being. This book maps onto the figure. Can it really be this simple? Yes, but *simple* doesn't mean *easy*. I invite you to use your nonjudgmental *self-awareness* to detect your current experience; to use your *attention control* (concentration), developed through meditation, to focus on your experience; and *emotion regulation* to manage the challenges that arise and to foster flourishing in yourself. You can then apply these three skills of self-regulation (attention control, self-awareness, and emotion regulation) to whatever arises in your life that can influence your well-being, such as your relationship to physical activity, diet, social relationships, sleep, stress, or whatever is coming up in yourself or in your social, political, or physical environment. Each of us has a different pathway to well-being. I encourage you to allow your journey to best match who you are and to respond skillfully to the environment you find yourself in. In remembering the definition of "mindfulness" in the introduction, where mindfulness is like an arrow, quickly bringing our wisdom to this very moment, what is here in your body, heart, mind, and spirit that is skillful to express now?

Perhaps consider this moment. Is there a way to apply this framework to your life in this moment? What is the biggest challenge or opportunity that you are facing? Can you apply the teachings—opening the body, opening the heart, opening the mind, and opening the spirit—to that specific challenge or opportunity right now? If it resonates with you, perhaps you can use the sixteen contemplations in the Discourse on the Breathing Mindfulness, such as liberating the mind (#12), impermanence (#14), or letting go (#16), to address this challenge or opportunity. Really. Right now. I invite you to pause and consider it for a few moments.

It is often tempting to think, *I'll learn about it now and apply it tomorrow.* But can you apply it right now? This moment is the only moment we ever have. The past is gone, and the future is yet to come.

If it seems wiser in this moment, can you just let be, knowing that you are perfect as you are? There are many causes and conditions that went into how you are in this flash of time. Can you pause, open toward this experience—this body and mind—and let it be just as it is? There is nothing we need to strive for. As shared earlier in this book, an element of mindfulness is the concept of nonstriving, or not grasping for an outcome in ways that take us away from ourselves in this moment. In many ways, this book is inviting you to just be you—to allow your natural self to come through and be expressed. Just be you, in this moment, and that is enough. In fact, it is wonderful.

The sculptor Michelangelo shared how he felt that before he started sculpting a block of marble, the sculpture was already complete. He just had to chisel away the superfluous material. It is like that with this book. Can what you learned here support you to let go of what isn't you and let your essence come through because that is who you are? In doing so, it will likely harness your greatest capacity to be yourself and serve society skillfully.

Sewing It All Together Meditation

The intention of this meditation is to provide you with a chance to take a step back and reflect on your original intentions and hopes when you started reading this book, what you experienced while reading this book, and where you would like to go from here.

Inviting you pause, even close your eyes, and ask yourself:

Why did I originally start reading this book?

What did I hope for?

What did I experience while reading the book?

What did I learn or discover, if anything?

What were the challenges I experienced while reading this book, and how did I work through them (if I did)?

How do I plan to move forward with mindfulness practice after this book is complete, if I plan to practice?

See if you can welcome all responses, even ones that are unsatisfactory. In this way, you are creating space to be here with what is being experienced and to create a platform to support you through change, as everything changes.

In the introduction, you were invited to answer questions about your mental and physical well-being and goals. I encourage you to flip back to them now and ask: How have things changed as a result of reading this book and practicing as you have? What were the main drivers that got you to that change, whether it was a positive or negative change, assuming there was a change (and if there was no change, what were the main causes of that)? What is resonating with you now in terms of where you have come on your life's journey during the process of reading this book and where you want to go next? This can be a good time to record any insights that arose for your future self.

As we do in MBSR and MBC, I invite you to write a letter to your future self, reflecting on what insights you had, what you learned, or what you want to remember. You may also want to set some short-term goals or intentions (that can be completed within a few weeks or months) and long-term goals or intentions (a few years out). I encourage you to consider writing about what might get in the way of those intentions and how you will work with that.

In the in-person class, we distribute envelopes and have students address the envelope, and then the teacher mails it to them at some point in the future (usually within six to twelve months). When the program is offered online, we invite students to write an email to themselves and schedule it to be sent six to twelve months in the future. They could also hand-write a letter to themselves and put it away somewhere, such as deep in a desk drawer, where they will find again sometime in the future. If you would like to, I invite you to write letter to yourself.

This letter writing exercise has some evidence behind it. It is used in behavioral medicine approaches, such as motivational interviewing, where patients set goals. They consider how motivated and confident they are to act on those goals, see what they can do to improve their motivation and confidence, consider what might get in the way of achieving the goals, what they will do if that happens, and then tell someone what those goals. Writing a letter to ourselves is a way of connecting with our future selves to remind us of insights about our life's priorities, values, and dreams.

Resources to Support You Moving Forward

There are three elements that support people to learn fast and well. If all three are present, learning can be remarkable. They are having (1) a teacher, (2) teachings (for example books or sheet music), and (3) a community to practice with. Consider something you have learned to a mastery level, whether it was piano, a sport, or math. Were all three elements present? For example, college, which many people are willing to pay tens of thousands of dollars a year to attend, provides teachers (professors), teachings (textbooks and digital presentations), and a community to practice with (classes with faculty, teaching assistants, other students, lab groups, study groups, departments, extracurricular-activity groups). When I learned to play mandolin, for example, I learned fastest and deeply when I had a teacher, some teachings (sheet music), and friends to jam with. With meditation and mindfulness, it's similar. Below are some resources for these three elements if you want to continue your journey beyond this book.

Teachers

There are, and have been, remarkable mindfulness and meditation teachers in the world, such as the Dalai Lama, Pema Chödron, Jon Kabat-Zinn, Sharon Salzberg, Joseph Goldstein, Bhante Gunaratana, Shunryu

Suzuki, Thich Nhat Hanh, Ajahn Chah, Eckhart Tolle, and many others (who have published books you could check out). For more teaching from me, you can check out the MBC app and the website for this book, http://www.newharbinger.com/49135 to access guided recordings and talks. There is also an online self-paced course called the Mindful College Student offered through the Omega Institute (https://www.eomega.org) that is complementary to this book. I occasionally lead live retreats and post free talks on YouTube. There are mindfulness apps, like Headspace and Unwinding Anxiety, with high-quality teachers like Andy Puddicombe and Jud Brewer. And, there are probably skilled teachers near you. Having a teacher whom you trust and respect, whom you can be in relationship with, and who can come to know you and learn your growth edges and then offer ideas for ways you can develop that you never would have known without them is infinitely valuable. I would not be who I am without the guidance of Joanne Friday, my teacher who recently passed away.

Teachings

Wonderful mindfulness teachings are in books and apps by the people mentioned in the section above, that you find valuable. Some of my favorite mindfulness books as a young adult were *Peace is Every Step* by Thich Nhat Hanh, *Awakening the Buddha Within* by Lama Surya Das, and *The Universe in a Single Atom: The Convergence of Science and Spirituality* by the Dalai Lama. Other respected mindfulness books often read by young adults include *The Mindful Twenty Something* by Dr. Holly Rogers and *Finding Peace in a Frantic World* by Dr. Mark Williams and Dr. Danny Penman.

Community

Having a mindfulness community is an incredibly helpful source of inspiration, ideas, friendship, and people to lift me up when I'm feeling down. It helps with the social pressure to be our best selves. If a group is meeting one night and they are looking forward to you being there, it's more likely you will go and personally benefit. If you take on a leadership role in the group, it's more likely that you will practice what you preach. I can't recommend enough finding your way to a community that practices mindfulness, maybe it is at church or spiritual center where it is woven into your belief system, as I have seen with a local mindfulness group that meets as part of a Jewish synagogue for example. You might even like to start a group in your community based on what you have learned in this and other books. The Mindfulness Center at Brown (http://brown.edu/mindfulnesscenter) offers many free live online mindfulness programs every week, and places like that can be a source of community too. There are so many options these days that it's highly probable you can find a mindfulness community that is a good match for your personality, either in-person or online.

The practices presented in this book are a framework, like frets and strings on a guitar. Just like anyone who learns to play guitar by understanding the frets, strings, and chords, you have learned a set of tools within this book. Everyone who learns to play the guitar, even those who master it, plays differently from anyone else. That is their unique sound with their personality coming through. I invite you to use the tools in this book to sing your song and be exactly who you already are.

Home Practice

While the ending of this book is indeed an ending, it is also the start of a new beginning: the next steps of your life's journey. You are invited to take the practices offered in this book and make them your own. Which ones work best for you? Recognizing that the most fruitful one isn't always the most comfortable, and sometimes it is. What practice leads you to notice positive shifts in your life? Keep in mind that the practices that are most

Acknowledgments

Just as in the dedication, I mentioned how the Haudenosaunee Confederacy (Iroquois) is attributed to considering the effects of their actions on seven generations in the future. In looking at the seven generations (and beyond) in the past, of my family, teachers, and the natural world, I am grateful for all that has allowed me to be able to write this book. I am also grateful for the current generations that surround me, including my wife Betsy and my twin eleven-year-old daughters, Monica and Stella, who understand the importance of this book, and gave me the support, space, time, inspiration, and emotional support to work on it. I am thankful to my mother, Dawn, for showing me the value of a spiritual life and ethics. I am grateful to my father, Barry, for always believing in my capacity to contribute to the world in skillful ways and letting me know when I might be in danger of not. My grandparents Andrew and Betty Gillespie modelled to me humor, wisdom, intelligence, culture, valuing friends and family, and not working so much that the richness of life is in danger of being lost. My grandparents Laura and Harold Loucks taught me the importance of planning ahead, hard work, resilience, nature, friends, family, and travel. I am indebted to my Buddhist and mindfulness teachers, particularly Thich Nhat Hanh, Joanne Friday, and Jon Kabat-Zinn, and I hope that their wisdom is shared skillfully in these pages to serve young adults well.

One of the reasons I research and teach mindfulness in a university setting is because of the quality of colleagues in academic mindfulness scholarship world-wide. There are too many to list, and just a few are Willem Kuyken, Sarah Shaw (both at Oxford University), Jud Brewer, Willoughby Britton, Lisa Uebelacker, Brandon Gaudiano, Jeff Proulx,

Shufang Sun, Jared Lindahl, Elena Salmoirago-Blotcher, Maggie Bublitz, Harold Roth (all at Brown University), Zev Schuman-Olivier, Carl Fulwiler and Sara Lazar (all at Harvard University), Becca Crane (Bangor University), Jean King (Worcester Polytechnic Institute), Liz Hoge (Georgetown University), Lone Fjorbaeck (Aaurhus University), Jayson Spas (Rhode Island College), and Dave Vago (Vanderbilt University and RoundGlass), to name just a few. The MBSR teacher-trainers and staff at the Mindfulness Center at Brown (such as Lynn Koerbel, Florence Melo-Meyer, Éowyn Ahlstrom, Patti Holland, Erin Woo, Bob Stahl, Jonathan Carlone, Colin Murphy, Dianne Horgan, Bill Nardi, and Frances Saadeh) along with members of the Global Mindfulness Collaborative, which is helping to deliver high-quality scalable MBSR teacher training around the world alongside other respected groups, have not only helped to inspire this book, but also shown me the importance of applying the research to communities with an emphasis on diversity and inclusion. Brown University is a fine institution to base this work out of, and its emphasis on interdisciplinarity, with a passion toward societal issues of import at this time, and an emphasis on rigorous research, has supported the development of the MBC program and the course Meditation, Mindfulness, and Health for without which this book would not have been written.

I am grateful to the community of literary experts that helped to bring this book to fruition, including my literary agent (Linda Konner), editors (Caleb Beckwith, Elizabeth Hollis-Hansen, Karen Chernyaev, Gretel Hakanson) and publisher New Harbinger Publications. And finally, thank you to the young adults and college students who encouraged me to develop MBC and the course Meditation, Mindfulness and Health in the formats they have become, and to all the young adults who have trusted me with sharing their stories in this book. As in chapter 4 where I mentioned the whole universe is in Betsy's and my wooden bureau, so too, the whole universe is in this book. May it be worth the trees from which the paper came from, and the resources the earth has provided, to publish it.

Recommended Levels of Health Behaviors

Fruits and Vegetables

The 2015–2020 Dietary Guidelines for Americans produced by the US Department of Health and Human Services and the US Department of Agriculture recommend making half your plate fruits and vegetables, as well as eating the equivalent of about two and a half cups of vegetables, and two cups of fruit per day, based on a two thousand calorie per day diet (amounts vary a little depending on body size) (US Department of Health and Human Services and US Department of Agriculture 2015).

Physical Activity

The US Department of Health and Human Services, in collaboration with the National Institutes of Health and the Centers for Disease Control, recommend that adults partake in at least two and half hours of moderate-intensity aerobic activity or one hour and fifteen minutes of vigorous-intensity aerobic activity every week as well as muscle-strengthening activities at least twice a week (US Department of Health and Human Services 2018).

Screen Time

The average amount of screen time in the US adults is about nine hours per day (The Nielsen Company 2018). High levels of screen time have been associated with risk for a range of psychosocial impacts, including depression and anxiety (Oswald et al. 2020). It is also related to physical health impacts, such as diabetes and obesity (Wu et al. 2016; Hu et al.

2003). You might note that I am not giving a number of screen time hours above which is harmful. This is still being researched, so I am hesitant to provide a number. However, the content of the screen time is important in assessing its impacts on our well-being.

Sleep

The American Academy of Sleep Medicine and the Sleep Research Society recommend that adults get at least seven hours of sleep a night (Watson et al. 2015).

Alcohol

The 2015–2020 Dietary Guidelines released by the US Department of Health and Human Services, in collaboration with the National Institutes of Health and the Centers for Disease Control, do not recommend that individuals begin drinking or drink more for any reason. If alcohol is consumed, it should be consumed in moderation—up to one drink per day for women and up to two drinks per day for men—and only by adults of legal drinking age (US Department of Health and Human Services 2018).

Tobacco Use

According to the 2020 Surgeon General's Report on Smoking Cessation, tobacco smoking remains the leading preventable cause of death and disease in the United Sates, and abstinence or reduction in smoking is encouraged (Office of the Surgeon General 2020). E-cigarettes are another matter. As of the time this book was written, e-cigarettes are still relatively new to the market, and while evidence suggests that e-cigarette vapor contains fewer toxicants than tobacco smoke, it still contains numerous toxicants due to the presence of nicotine, propylene glycol, glycerin, and metal contaminants (Bozier et al. 2020). We will better understand the effects of e-cigarettes on health as more high-quality studies are published in the coming years.

The Sixteen Contemplations in the Discourse on Breathing Mindfulness

Note: Some of the contemplations have been adapted for this book.

1. *Breathing in, I know I am breathing in. Breathing out, I know I am breathing out.*

2. *Breathing in a long breath or a short breath, I know whether it is a long breath or a short breath. Breathing out a long breath or a short breath, I know whether it is a long breath or a short breath.*

3. *Breathing in, I am aware of my whole body. Breathing out, I am aware of my whole body.*

4. *Breathing in, I calm my body. Breathing out, I care for my body.*

5. *Breathing in, I feel joyful. Breathing out, I feel joyful.*

6. *Breathing in, I feel happy. Breathing out, I feel happy.*

7. *Breathing in, I am aware of my mental formations (emotions). Breathing out, I am aware of my mental formations.*

8. *Breathing in, I calm my mental formations (emotions). Breathing out, I care for my mental formations.*

9. *Breathing in, I am aware of my mind (citta). Breathing out, I am aware of my mind.*

10. *Breathing in, I gladden my mind. Breathing out, I gladden my mind.*

11. *Breathing in, I concentrate my mind. Breathing out, I concentrate my mind.*

12. *Breathing in, I liberate my mind. Breathing out, I liberate my mind.*

13. *Breathing in, I observe the impermanent nature of all phenomena. Breathing out, I observe the impermanent nature of all phenomena.*

14. *Breathing in, I observe the disappearance of desire. Breathing out, I observe the disappearance of desire.*

15. *Breathing in, I observe cessation. Breathing out, I observe cessation.*

16. *Breathing in, I observe letting go. Breathing out, I observe letting go.*

References

Analāyo, Bhikkhu. 2019. *Mindfulness of Breathing.* Cambridge, UK: Windhorse Publications.

Anderson, N. B., C. D. Belar, S. J. Breckler, K. C. Nordal, D. W. Ballard, L. F. Bufka, L. Bossolo, S. Bethune, A. Brownawell, and K. Wiggins. 2014. "Stress in America: Are Teens Adopting Adults' Stress Habits?" February 14. http://stressinamerica.org.

Baer, R., C. Crane, E. Miller, and W. Kuyken. 2019. "Doing No Harm in Mindfulness-Based Programs: Conceptual Issues and Empirical Findings." *Clinical Psychology Review* 71: 101–114. https://doi.org/10.1016/j.cpr.2019.01.001.

Bozier, J., E. K. Chivers, D. G. Chapman, A. N. Larcombe, N. A. Bastian, J. A. Masso-Silva, M. K. Byun, C. F. McDonald, L. E. Crotty Alexander, and M. P. Ween. 2020. "The Evolving Landscape of e-Cigarettes: A Systematic Review of Recent Evidence." *Chest* 157 (5): 1362–1390. https://doi.org/10.1016/j.chest.2019.12.042.

Bratman, G. N., J. P. Hamilton, and G. C. Daily. 2012. "The Impacts of Nature Experience on Human Cognitive Function and Mental Health." *Annals of New York Academy of Sciences* 1249: 118–136. https://doi.org/10.1111/j.1749-6632.2011.06400.x.

Brewer, J. A., P. D Worhunsky, J. R Gray, Y. Y. Tang, J. Weber, and H. Kober. 2011. "Meditation Experience Is Associated with Differences in Default Mode Network Activity and Connectivity. " *Proceedings of the National Academy of Sciences of the United States of America* 108, no. 50: 20254–20259. https://doi.org/10.1073/pnas.1112029108.

Brumage, M., and M. Gross. 2015. "In the Moment." *Training and Conditioning.* December.

Buddhadāsa Bhikkhu. 1987. "Using *Ānāpānasati-Bhāvanā* for Daily Life," translated by Santikaro Bhikkhu. October 10. http://www.bia.or.th/en/index.php/teachings-by-buddhadasa-bhikkhu/transcripts/suan-mokkh-retreats-1987/send/22-1987/247-using-anapanasati-bhavana-for-daily-life.

———. 1988. *Mindfulness With Breathing: A Manual for Serious Beginners.* Somerville, MA: Wisdom Publications.

Buysse, D. J., C. F. Reynolds III, T. H. Monk, S. R. Berman, and D. J. Kupfer. 1989. "The Pittsburgh Sleep Quality Index: A New Instrument for Psychiatric Practice and Research." *Psychiatry Research* 28, no. 2: 193–213. http://www.ncbi.nlm.nih.gov/pubmed/2748771.

Center for Collegiate Mental Health. 2021. "2020 Annual Report (Publication No. STA 21-045)."

Christakis, N. A., and J. H. Fowler. 2007. "The Spread of Obesity in a Large Social Network over 32 Years." *New England Journal of Medicine* 357, no. 4: 370–379. http://www.ncbi.nlm.nih.gov/entrez/query.fcgi?cmd =Retrieve&db=PubMed&dopt=Citation&list_uids=17652652.

————. 2008. "The Collective Dynamics of Smoking in a Large Social Network." *New England Journal of Medicine* 358, no. 21: 2249–2258. https://doi.org/10.1056/NEJMsa0706154. https://www.ncbi.nlm.nih .gov/pubmed/18499567.

Cohen, S., T. Kamarck, and R. Mermelstein. 1983. "A Global Measure of Perceived Stress." *Journal of Health and Social Behavior* 24, no. 4: 385–396. http://www.ncbi.nlm.nih.gov/entrez/query.fcgi?cmd=Retrieve&db =PubMed&dopt=Citation&list_uids=6668417.

Craig, C. L., A. L. Marshall, M. Sjöström, A. E. Bauman, M. L. Booth, B. E. Ainsworth, M. Pratt, U. Ekelund, A. Yngve, J. F. Sallis, and P. Oja. 2003. "International Physical Activity Questionnaire: 12-Country Reliability and Validity." *Medicine and Science in Sports and Exercise* 35, no. 8: 1381–1395. https://doi.org/10.1249/01.MSS.0000078924.61453.FB.

Cullen, B., K. Eichel, J. R. Lindahl, H. Rahrig, N. Kini, J. Flahive, and W. B. Britton. 2021. "The Contributions of Focused Attention and Open Monitoring in Mindfulness-Based Cognitive Therapy for Affective Disturbances: A 3-Armed Randomized Dismantling Trial." *PLOS ONE* 16, no. 1: e0244838. https://doi.org/10.1371/journal.pone.0244838.

Dawson, A. F., W. W. Brown, J. Anderson, B. Datta, J. N. Donald, K. Hong, S. Allan, T. B. Mole, P. B. Jones, and J. Galante. 2019. "Mindfulness-Based Interventions for University Students: A Systematic Review and Meta-Analysis of Randomised Controlled Trials." *Applied Psychology: Health and Well-Being*. https://doi.org/10.1111/aphw.12188.

de Vibe, M., A. Bjørndal, S. Fattah, G. M. Dyrdal, E. Halland, and E. E. Tanner-Smitth. 2017. "Mindfulness-Based Stress Reduction (MBSR) for Improving Health, Quality of Life and Social Functioning in Adults: A Systematic Review and Meta-Analysis." *Campbell Systematic Reviews* 13, no. 1: 1–264.

Djernis, D., I. Lerstrup, D., Poulsen, U. Stigsdotter, J. Dahlgaard, and M. O'Toole. 2019. "A Systematic Review and Meta-Analysis of Nature-Based Mindfulness: Effects of Moving Mindfulness Training into an Outdoor Natural Setting." *International Journal of Environmental Research and Public Health* 16, no. 17. https://doi.org/10.3390/ijerph16173202.

Feldman, C., and W. Kuyken. 2019. *Mindfulness: Ancient Wisdom Meets Modern Psychology.* New York: The Guilford Press.

Fowler, J. H., and N. A. Christakis. 2008. "Dynamic Spread of Happiness in a Large Social Network: Longitudinal Analysis over 20 years in the Framingham Heart Study." *BMJ* 337: a2338. https://doi.org/10.1136/bmj.a2338.

Gaudiano, B. A., S. Ellenberg, B. Ostrove, J. Johnson, K. T. Mueser, M. Furman, and I. W. Miller. 2020. "Feasibility and Preliminary Effects of Implementing Acceptance and Commitment Therapy for Inpatients With Psychotic-Spectrum Disorders in a Clinical Psychiatric Intensive Care Setting." *Journal of Cognitive Psychotherapy* 34, no. 1: 80–96. https://doi.org/10.1891/0889-8391.34.1.80.

Gaultney, J. F. 2010. "The Prevalence of Sleep Disorders in College Students: Impact on Academic Performance." *Journal of American College Health* 59, no. 2: 91–97. https://doi.org/10.1080/07448481.2010.483708.

Gerritsen, R. J. S., and G. P. H. Band. 2018. "Breath of Life: The Respiratory Vagal Stimulation Model of Contemplative Activity." *Frontiers in Human Neuroscience* 12: 397. https://doi.org/10.3389/fnhum.2018.00397.

Gethin, R. 2015. "Buddhist Conceptualizations of Mindfulness." In *Handbook of Mindfulness* edited by K. W. Brown, J. D. Creswell, and R. M. Ryan. New York: The Guilford Press.

Gilbert, S. F. 2000. *Developmental Biology*, 6th ed. Sunderland, MA: Sinauer Associates.

Gotink, R. A., R. Meijboom, M. W. Vernooij, M. Smits, and M. G. Hunink. 2016. "8-Week Mindfulness-Based Stress Reduction Induces Brain Changes Similar to Traditional Long-Term Meditation Practice— A Systematic Review." *Brain and Cognition* 108: 32–41. https://doi.org/10.1016/j.bandc.2016.07.001.

Gu, J., C. Strauss, R. Bond, and K. Cavanagh. 2015. "How Do Mindfulness-Based Cognitive Therapy and Mindfulness-Based Stress Reduction Improve Mental Health and Wellbeing? A Systematic Review and Meta-Analysis of Mediation Studies." *Clinical Psychology Review* 37: 1–12. https://doi.org/10.1016/j.cpr.2015.01.006.

Hu, F. B., T. Y. Li, G. A. Colditz, W. C. Willett, and J. E. Manson. 2003. "Television Watching and Other Sedentary Behaviors in Relation to Risk of Obesity and Type 2 diabetes Mellitus in Women." *JAMA* 289, no. 14: 1785–1791. https://doi.org/10.1001/jama.289.14.1785.

Incze, M., R. F. Redberg, and A. Gupta. 2018. "I Have Insomnia—What Should I Do?" *JAMA Internal Medicine* 178, no. 11: 1572. https://doi.org/10.1001/jamainternmed.2018.2626.

Kabat-Zinn, J. 2013. *Full Catastrophe Living: Using the Wisdom of your Body and Mind to Face Stress, Pain, and Illness.* New York: Bantam.

Kabat-Zinn, J. 2021. Personal communication.

Kuyken, W., F. C. Warren, R. S. Taylor, B. Whalley, C. Crane, G. Bondolfi, R. Hayes, M. Huijbers, H. Ma, S. Schweizer, Z. Segal, A. Speckens, J. D. Teasdale, K. Van Heeringen, M. Williams, S. Byford, R. Byng, and T. Dalgleish. 2016. "Efficacy of Mindfulness-Based Cognitive Therapy in Prevention of Depressive Relapse: An Individual Patient Data Meta-analysis From Randomized Trials." *JAMA Psychiatry* 73, no. 6: 565–574. https://doi.org/10.1001/jamapsychiatry.2016.0076.

Li, D., and W. C. Sullivan. 2016. "Impact of Views to School Landscapes on Recovery from Stress and Mental Fatigue." *Landscape and Urban Planning* 148: 149–158.

Lindahl, J. R., N. E. Fisher, D. J. Cooper, R. K. Rosen, and W. B. Britton. 2017. "The Varieties of Contemplative Experience: A Mixed-Methods Study of Meditation-Related Challenges in Western Buddhists." *PLoS One* 12, no. 5: e0176239. https://doi.org/10.1371/journal.pone.0176239.

Lomas, T., N. Etcoff, W. Van Gordon, and E. Shonin. 2017. "Zen and the Art of Living Mindfully: The Health-Enhancing Potential of Zen Aesthetics." *Journal of Religion and Health* 56, no. 5: 1720–1739. https://doi.org10.1007/s10943-017-0446-5.

Loucks, E. B., W. R. Nardi, R. Gutman, I. M. Kronish, F. B. Saadeh, Y. Li, et al. 2019. "Mindfulness-Based Blood Pressure Reduction (MB-BP): Stage 1 Single-Arm Clinical Trial." *PLoS One* 14, no. 11: e0223095. https://doi.org/10.1371/journal.pone.0223095.

Loucks, E. B., W. R. Nardi, R. Gutman, F. B. Saadeh, Y. Li, D. R. Vago, L. B. Fiske, J. J. Spas, and A. Harrison. 2021. "Mindfulness-Based College: A Stage 1 Randomized Controlled Trial for University Student Well-Being." *Psychosomatic Medicine* 83, no. 6: 602–614. https://doi.org/10.1097/PSY.0000000000000860.

Molendijk, M., P. Molero, F. Ortuno Sánchez-Pedreño, W. Van der Does, and M. Angel Martínez-González. 2018. "Diet Quality and Depression Risk: A Systematic Review and Dose-Response Meta-Analysis of Prospective Studies." *Journal of Affective Disorders* 226: 346–354. https://doi.org/10 .1016/j.jad.2017.09.022.

Muth, J. J. *Zen Shorts.* 2005. New York: Scholastic Press.

Nardi, W. R., A. Harrison, F. B. Saadeh, J. Webb, A. E. Wentz, and E. B. Loucks. 2020. "Mindfulness and Cardiovascular Health: Qualitative Findings on Mechanisms from the Mindfulness-Based Blood Pressure Peduction (MB-BP) Study." *PLOS ONE* 15, no. 9: e0239533. https://doi .org/10.1371/journal.pone.0239533.

National Institute on Drug Abuse. 2019. "NIDA-Modified ASSIST Questionnaire." http://www.drugabuse.gov/sites/default/files/pdf/nmassist.pdf.

Nielsen Company, The. 2018. "The Nielsen Total Audience Report: Q1: 2018."

Nhat Hanh, T. 1987. *Old Path, White Clouds: Walking in the Footsteps of the Buddha.* Berkeley, CA: Parallax Press.

———. 1991. *Peace is Every Step: The Path of Mindfulness in Everyday Life.* New York: Bantam Books.

———. 1998. *In the Heart of the Buddha's Teachings.* New York: Broadway Books.

———. 2007. *Chanting from the Heart: Buddhist Ceremonies and Daily Practices* edited by T. N. Hanh. Berkeley, CA: Parallax Press.

———. 2008. *Breathe, You Are Alive! Sutra on the Full Awareness of Breathing.* Berkeley, CA: Parallax Press.

Office of the Surgeon General. 2020. "Smoking Cessation: A Report of the Surgeon General." In Publications and Reports of the Surgeon General. Washington, DC.

Oswald, T. K., A. R. Rumbold, S. G. E. Kedzior, and V. M. Moore. 2020. "Psychological Impacts of 'Screen Time' and 'Green Time' for Children and Adolescents: A Systematic Scoping Review." *PLOS ONE* 15, no. 9: e0237725. https://doi.org/10.1371/journal.pone.0237725.

Parsons, C. E., C. Crane, J. L. Parsons, L. O. Fjorback, and W. Kuyken. 2017. "Home Practice in Mindfulness-Based Cognitive Therapy and Mindfulness-Based Stress Reduction: A Systematic Review and Meta-Analysis of Participants' Mindfulness Practice and Its Association with Outcomes." *Behaviour Research and Therapy* 95: 29–41. https://doi.org/10.1016/j.brat .2017.05.004.

Pollan, M. 2007. "Unhappy Meals." *New York Times Magazine*, January 28.

Rosenberg, L. 1998. *Breath by Breath: The Liberating Practice of Insight Meditation.* Boulder, CO: Shambala Publications, Inc.

Salzberg, S. 2002. *Loving-Kindness: The Revolutionary Art of Happiness.* Boulder, CO: Shambala Publications, Inc.

Segal, Z. V., J. M. G. Williams, and J. D. Teasdale. 2012. *Mindfulness-Based Cognitive Therapy for Depression.* New York: The Guildford Press.

Shaw, S. 2006. *Buddhist Meditation: An Anthology of Texts from the Pāli Canon.* Milton Park, England: Routledge.

Smith, P. C., S. M. Schmidt, D. Allensworth-Davies, and R. Saitz. 2010. "A Single-Question Screening Test for Drug Use in Primary Care." *Archives of Internal Medicine* 170, no. 13: 1155–1160. https://doi.org/10.1001/archinternmed.2010.140.

Sotos-Prieto, M., S. N. Bhupathiraju, J. Mattei, T. T. Fung, Y. Li, A. Pan, W. C. Willett, E. B. Rimm, and F. B. Hu. 2017. "Association of Changes in Diet Quality with Total and Cause-Specific Mortality." *New England Journal of Medicine* 377, no. 2: 143–153. https://doi.org/10.1056/NEJMoa1613502.

Subar, A. F., F. E. Thompson, V. Kipnis, D. Midthune, P. Hurwitz, S. McNutt, A. McIntosh, and S. Rosenfeld. 2001. "Comparative Validation of the Block, Willett, and National Cancer Institute Food Frequency Questionnaires: The Eating at America's Table Study." *American Journal of Epidemiology* 154, no. 12: 1089–1099. http://www.ncbi.nlm.nih.gov/entrez/query.fcgi?cmd=Retrieve&db=PubMed&dopt=Citation&list_uids=11744511.

Tang, Y. Y., B. K. Hölzel, and M. I. Posner. 2015. "The Neuroscience of Mindfulness Meditation." *Nature Reviews Neuroscience* 16, no. 4: 213–225. https://doi.org/10.1038/nrn3916.

Thomas, M. C., T. W. Kamarck, X. Li, K. I. Erickson, and S. B. Manuck. 2019. "Physical Activity Moderates the Effects of Daily Psychosocial Stressors on Ambulatory Blood Pressure." *Health Psychology* 10: 925–935. https://doi.org/10.1037/hea0000755.

Throuvala, M. A., M. D. Griffiths, M. Rennoldson, and D. J. Kuss. 2020. "Mind over Matter: Testing the Efficacy of an Online Randomized Controlled Trial to Reduce Distraction from Smartphone Use." *International Journal of Environmental Research and Public Health* 17, no. 13. https://doi.org/10.3390/ijerph17134842.

Treleaven, D. A. 2018. *Trauma-Sensitive Mindfulness: Practices for Safe and Transformative Healing.* New York: W. W. Norton & Company.

Twenge, J. M., B. Gentile, C. N. DeWall, D. Ma, K. Lacefield, and D. R. Schurtz. 2010. "Birth Cohort Increases in Psychopathology among Young Americans, 1938–2007: A Cross-Temporal Meta-Analysis of the MMPI." *Clinical Psychology Review* 30, no. 2: 145–154. https://doi.org/10 .1016/j.cpr.2009.10.005.

US Department of Health and Human Services. 2018. "Physical Activity Guidelines for Americans, 2nd Edition." Washington, DC.

US Department of Health and Human Services, and U.S. Department of Agriculture. 2015. "2015–2020 Dietary Guidelines for Americans. 8th Edition."

Vizcaino, M., M. Buman, C. T. DesRoches, and C. Wharton. 2019. "Reliability of a New Measure to Assess Modern Screen Time in Adults." *BMC Public Health* 19, no. 1: 1386. https://doi.org/10.1186/s12889-019 -7745-6.

Watson, N. F., M. S. Badr, G. Belenky, D. L. Bliwise, O. M. Buxton, D. Buysse, et al. 2015. "Recommended Amount of Sleep for a Healthy Adult: A Joint Consensus Statement of the American Academy of Sleep Medicine and Sleep Research Society." *Sleep* 38, no. 6: 843–844. https:// doi.org/10.5665/sleep.4716.

Watts, A. 1951. *The Way of Zen.* New York: Pantheon Books.

White, R. L., M. J. Babic, P. D. Parker, D. R. Lubans, T. Astell-Burt, and C. Lonsdale. 2017. "Domain-Specific Physical Activity and Mental Health: A Meta-Analysis." *American Journal of Preventive Medicine* 52, no. 5: 653–666. https://doi.org/10.1016/j.amepre.2016.12.008.

Willett, W. C., L. Sampson, M. J. Stampfer, B. Rosner, C. Bain, J. Witschi, C. H. Hennekens, and F. E. Speizer. 1985. "Reproducibility and Validity of a Semiquantitative Food Frequency Questionnaire." *American Journal of Epidemiology* 122, no. 1: 51–65. http://www.ncbi.nlm.nih.gov/entrez/query .fcgi?cmd=Retrieve&db=PubMed&dopt=Citation&list_uids=4014201.

World Health Organization. 1948. *Constitution of the World Health Organization.*

Wu, L., S. Sun, Y. He, and B. Jiang. 2016. "The Effect of Interventions Targeting Screen Time Reduction: A Systematic Review and Meta-Analysis." *Medicine (Baltimore)* 95, no. 27: e4029. https://doi.org/10.1097 /MD.0000000000004029.

Endnotes

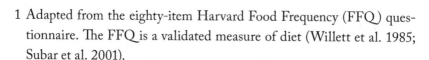

1 Adapted from the eighty-item Harvard Food Frequency (FFQ) questionnaire. The FFQ is a validated measure of diet (Willett et al. 1985; Subar et al. 2001).

2 Adapted from the eighty-item Harvard Food Frequency (FFQ) questionnaire. The FFQ is a validated measure of diet (Willett et al. 1985; Subar et al. 2001).

3 Adapted from the International Physical Activity Questionnaire (IPAQ). The IPAQ is a validated measure of physical activity (Craig et al. 2003), recognizing it's not easy to accurately measure physical activity, and actigraphy is another recommended approach.

4 Adapted from the Vizcaino screen time questionnaire. This questionnaire has been validated (Vizcaino et al. 2019), and you might like to take the full questionnaire if you'd like the measure to be more accurate. Even more accurate is using an app to measure the screen time directly.

5 Adapted from the validated Pittsburgh Sleep Quality Index, and you may like to take the full questionnaire there if you'd like the measure to be more accurate (Buysse et al. 1989).

6 Adapted from Perceived Stress Scale (Cohen et al. 1983), and you may like to take the full questionnaire if you'd like the measure to be more accurate.

7 Adapted from National Institute on Drug Abuse Quick Screen v1.0 (Smith et al. 2010; National Institute on Drug Abuse 2019), and you may like to take the full questionnaire if you'd like the measure to be more accurate.

8 The trial randomly assigned forty-seven people to MBC and forty-nine people to an enhanced usual care control group. Both groups were offered a referral to the study's psychiatrist and university counseling resources if they had clinical levels of anxiety, depression, or suicidal ideation.

Eric B. Loucks, PhD, is a professor, researcher, speaker, and pioneer in the study of mindfulness and health. As director of the Mindfulness Center at Brown University—one of the premier research- and education-focused mindfulness centers in the world—Loucks teaches mindfulness-based programs and leads high-quality, methodologically rigorous research to investigate the science behind mindfulness and its impact on health and well-being. An expert in aging-related research, he optimizes mindfulness programs to specific age groups. He is lead developer of Mindfulness-Based College (MBC), and has received research grants from the National Institutes of Health to evaluate the effectiveness of mindfulness-based programs, including MBC and MB-BP. Over the course of his career, he has held teaching positions at Harvard, McGill, and Brown Universities. Loucks has practiced mindfulness for more than twenty years and received ordination in the Vietnamese Zen tradition of Thich Nhat Hanh.

Foreword writer **Judson A. Brewer, MD, PhD,** is director of research and innovation at the Mindfulness Center, and associate professor in behavioral and social sciences at the School of Public Health and Psychiatry at Brown University School of Medicine. A psychiatrist and internationally known expert in mindfulness training for addictions, he is author of *The Craving Mind* and *Unwinding Anxiety*. Follow him on twitter @judbrewer.

Real change *is* possible

For more than forty-five years, New Harbinger has published proven-effective self-help books and pioneering workbooks to help readers of all ages and backgrounds improve mental health and well-being, and achieve lasting personal growth. In addition, our spirituality books offer profound guidance for deepening awareness and cultivating healing, self-discovery, and fulfillment.

Founded by psychologist Matthew McKay and Patrick Fanning, New Harbinger is proud to be an independent, employee-owned company. Our books reflect our core values of integrity, innovation, commitment, sustainability, compassion, and trust. Written by leaders in the field and recommended by therapists worldwide, New Harbinger books are practical, accessible, and provide real tools for real change.

 **newharbinger**publications

MORE BOOKS from
NEW HARBINGER PUBLICATIONS

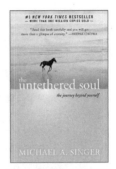

Did you know there are **free tools** you can download for this book?

Free tools are things like **worksheets, guided meditation exercises**, and **more** that will help you get the most out of your book.

You can download free tools for this book—whether you bought or borrowed it, in any format, from any source—from the New Harbinger website. All you need is a NewHarbinger.com account. Just use the URL provided in this book to view the free tools that are available for it. Then, click on the "download" button for the free tool you want, and follow the prompts that appear to log in to your NewHarbinger.com account and download the material.

You can also save the free tools for this book to your **Free Tools Library** so you can access them again anytime, just by logging in to your account! Just look for this button on the book's free tools page.

+ Save this to my free tools library

If you need help accessing or downloading free tools, visit **newharbinger.com/faq** or contact us at **customerservice@newharbinger.com**.